STUDY TEXT

Introduction to Securities and Investment

Syllabus version 10

In this July 2010 edition

- A **user-friendly format** for easy navigation
- **Exam tips** to put you on the right track
- A **Test your Knowledge** quiz at the end of each chapter
- A full **Index**

APPROVED WORKBOOK

Published July 2010

ISBN 9780 7517 8164 9

British Library Cataloguing-in-Publication Data
A catalogue record for this book
is available from the British Library

Published by

BPP Learning Media Ltd
BPP House, Aldine Place
London W12 8AA

www.bpp.com/learningmedia

Printed in Great Britain

Your learning materials, published by BPP Learning Media Ltd, are printed on paper sourced from sustainable, managed forests.

A note about copyright

Dear Customer

What does the little © mean and why does it matter?
Your market-leading BPP books, course materials
and e-learning materials do not write and update
themselves. People write them: on their own behalf
or as employees of an organisation that invests in
this activity. Copyright law protects their livelihoods.
It does so by creating rights over the use of the
content.
Breach of copyright is a form of theft – as well being
a criminal offence in some jurisdictions, it is
potentially a serious beach of professional ethics.

With current technology, things might seem a bit
hazy but, basically, without the express permission
of BPP Learning Media:

- Photocopying our materials is a breach of
  copyright
- Scanning, ripcasting or conversion of our
  digital materials into different file formats,
  uploading them to facebook or emailing
  them to your friends is a breach of
  copyright

You can, of course, sell your books, in the form in
which you have brought them – once you have
finished with them. (Is this fair to your fellow
students? We update for a reason.) But the
e-products are sold on a single user license basis:
we do not supply 'unlock' codes to people who have
bought them second-hand.

And what about outside the UK? BPP Learning Media
strives to make our materials available at prices
students can afford by local printing arrangements,
pricing policies and partnerships which are clearly
listed on our website. A tiny minority ignore this and
indulge in criminal activity by illegally photocopying
out material or supporting organisations that do. If
they act illegally and unethically in one area, can you
really trust them?

CONTENTS

Chapter 1   Page 1

Financial Services and the Economic Environment

Chapter 2   Page 25

Asset Classes

Chapter 3   Page 59

Derivatives

Chapter 4   Page 73

Financial Products

Chapter 5   Page 91

Pooled Investment Funds

Chapter 6   Page 109

Investment Wrappers

Chapter 7   Page 117

Financial Services Regulation

Chapter 8   Page 141

Taxation and Trusts

Index   Page 155

1

Financial Services and the Economic Environment

INTRODUCTION

In this chapter, we start with an overview of the analysis of the economy. We consider the measurement of inflation and the determination of interest rates.

We look at the role of central banks (for the UK, the Bank of England).

We will outline other key types of institution in the UK financial services sector and in major markets around the world.

Effectively functioning exchanges and markets are important to ensure an efficient financial sector, and we shall explain the role of the London Stock Exchange and other financial marketplaces.

CHAPTER CONTENTS

Page

1   The Economic Environment 4
2   The Bank of England...9
3   Financial Institutions 10
4   The London Stock Exchange 14
5   Derivatives and Commodity Markets 16
6   World Securities Markets...17
7   Foreign Exchange 18
8   Retail and Professional Business 20
9   Investment Distribution Channels 20
Chapter Roundup...22
Test Your Knowledge 23

1

CHAPTER LEARNING OBJECTIVES

Economic Environment

- **Know** the factors which determine the level of economic activity:

  - State-controlled economies
  - Market economies
  - Mixed economies
  - Open economies

- **Know** the functions of the Bank of England

- **Know** the functions of the Monetary Policy Committee

- **Know** how goods and services are paid for and how credit is created

- **Understand** the impact of inflation on economic behaviour

- **Know** the meaning of the following measures of inflation:

  - Retail Price Index
  - RPIX
  - Consumer Prices Index

- **Know** the impact of the following economic data:

  - Gross Domestic Product (GDP)
  - Balance of Payments
  - Public Sector Net Cash Requirement (PSNCR)
  - Level of unemployment

The Financial Services Industry

- **Know** the role of the following within the financial services industry:

  - Retail banks
  - Building societies
  - Investment banks
  - Pension funds
  - Insurance companies
  - Fund managers
  - Stockbrokers
  - Custodians
  - Third party administrators (TPAs)
  - Industry trade and professional bodies

- **Know** the function of and differences between retail and professional business and who the main customers are in each case:

  - Retail clients and professional clients

- **Know** the role of the following investment distribution channels:
    - Independent Financial Adviser
    - Tied Adviser
    - Platforms
    - Execution only

Foreign Exchange Market

- **Know** the basic structure of the foreign exchange market including spot and forward rates

Derivatives/Commodity Markets

- **Know** the characteristics of the derivatives and commodity markets:
    - Trading (metals, energy)

- **Know** the advantages and disadvantages of investing in the derivatives and commodity markets

World Stock Markets

- **Know** the characteristics of the following exchanges:
    - London Stock Exchange
    - New York Stock Exchange
    - NASDAQ
    - Euronext
    - Tokyo Stock Exchange
    - Deutsche Börse

Equities

- **Know** the difference between the primary market and secondary market

1 THE ECONOMIC ENVIRONMENT

Learning objective | **Know** the factors which determine the level of economic activity; state-controlled economies; market economies; mixed economies; open economies

1.1 Macroeconomics

Macroeconomics considers the study of the economy as a whole, looking at the various input factors, and resultant output, of both goods and services.

The simplest model to understanding how a macroeconomy works is to look at the theory of circular flows. In this model, we consider just two groups within an economy: the households, who own the productive assets or factor inputs of the economy (land, labour and capital), and the firms who employ these resources.

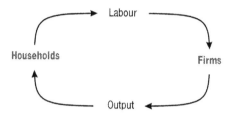

Households provide their labour in exchange for money (income). In turn, the households then spend this money on goods produced by the firms. Ultimately, since the firms are owned by the households, all value produced within the firms belongs to the households and are returned to them via the factor income. For the system to be in state of balance (equilibrium) the flows must be equal, i.e. the market must clear.

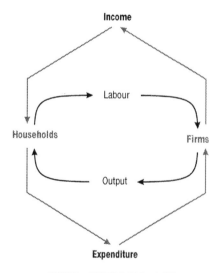

OUTPUT = EXPENDITURE = INCOME

1.2 State controlled economies

In a centrally planned, **State-controlled economy**, economic decisions are made by the central government. The State decides which goods will be produced, how these goods will be produced and how much each person will receive. Since individuals make no decisions, there are no real incentives for efficiency in production methods, or for goods to be made with the aim of making a profit. State controlled economies, such as those that used to exist in Eastern Europe and the former Soviet Union, saw little success through following such a centralised policy.

1.3 Market economies

In a **market economy**, the dynamic forces of supply and demand determine which goods will be produced and how many of each type. In other words, production is driven both by what firms believe people want to buy, and by the products that earn producers the highest profits. Hence, in market economies an element of competition and financial reward are key factors in influencing the level of economic activity. Firms which do not adapt to changing consumer desires, by producing goods which meet these desires, will fail.

1.4 Mixed economies

Some economies, such as the United Kingdom, show elements of competing market forces as well as some intervention by the State, and this is called a **mixed economy**. This is based on the notion that there are 'public goods', meaning goods that would not be provided in optimal amounts if left solely to the private sector. So, the State makes some provision to provide for the basic needs of the population – things like education, defence and transport. The allocations of funds for the provision of these basic services are made by the Chancellor of the Exchequer, who is head of the Treasury.

A competitive element is also present in the economy in the form of contracts put out to tender in the private sector. An example of the private sector working in conjunction with the public sector in the provision of basic services would include contracts for hospital catering or cleaning. The actual function would be carried out by the private contractor, having successfully won the contract by taking part in a competitive bidding process, whilst the supervisory role would be maintained by the local government authority.

1.5 Open economies

The term '**open economy**' refers to economies where there are few restrictions to foreign companies wishing to establish themselves in the domestic market. Barriers to entry could include high initial start-up costs and a heavy tax regime for non-local competitors, both of which will act as a disincentive to new players from abroad wishing to enter the local scene.

Within Europe, economic integration across Europe has moved closer with the removal of barriers within markets, such as tariffs, by facilitating labour market mobility through recognition of qualifications across the EU, and also by some moves towards harmonisation of tax rates such as value added tax. In the financial services sector, the **Markets in Financial Instruments Directive (MiFID)** has had, as one of its aims, the facilitation of cross-border provision of financial services within Europe.

1.6 Exchange rates

Cross-border transactions give rise to the issue of exchange rates. An exchange rate can simply be thought of as the price of one country's currency in terms of another country's currency.

In many cases, this price is determined by dynamic market forces and, hence, is known as a **floating exchange rate**. Factors which have an influence on exchange rates include relative purchasing power of money in the two currencies, general economic performance and relative interest rates.

The **euro** replaced individual currencies within much of European Union during 2002, thus creating a single currency for the Eurozone. This not only eliminated any exchange rate movements and associated currency risk for trade within that zone, but also removed significant differences in interest rates between Eurozone member countries.

Example: Exchange rates

Consider the following scenario. Suppose that a basket of goods in the UK currently costs £100. In the US, the same basket of goods costs $145. Suppose that the exchange rate between the UK and US is £1 = $1.45. Let us assume that prices in the UK rise (UK domestic inflation) and the same basket of goods in the UK now costs £115, while prices in the US remain static. The new exchange rate which preserves the same purchasing power in each currency is now £1 = $1.26. In other words, the value of sterling has declined (or looking at it another way, the value of the dollar (i.e. 1.45/1.15) has strengthened).

Under a floating exchange rate system, the price of a currency is allowed to move in response to changes in the underlying economy. Relative rates of inflation is one such change that can influence exchange rates. However, some countries choose to fix or peg their currency to a major world currency such as the US$, or to a basket of currencies. This means that the country's currency has a fixed rate or range, within which it is kept through action by the central authorities.

Exam tip	You will not be required to perform any exchange rate calculations in the exam.

1.7 Payments for goods and credit creation

Learning objective	**Know** how goods and services are paid for and how credit is created

Goods are generally paid for either at the point of sale, or through a credit mechanism, when the actual cash is paid at a later date. As a result, there are times when individuals spend more than they currently have, thus creating an increase in consumption levels.

Since both actual cash in circulation (notes and coins) and credit (a sum of money lent by the banking system) allow for spending, the mechanism by which banks lend money to fund spending further increases the supply of money in the economy. Banks usually keep around 10% of deposits as a reserve, leaving the remainder to lend out to other customers. Assuming these individuals place some, if not all, of this money into deposit accounts, the process continues, with banks keeping 10% in reserve and lending out the rest. In this way credit creation is part of the process through which the money supply is expanded. It is commercial banks that are involved in the process of credit creation.

If there is 'too much money chasing too few goods', as monetarist economists have described it, this may lead to **inflation**.

1.8 Inflation

Learning objectives	**Understand** the impact of inflation on economic behaviour **Know** the meaning of the following measures of inflation: Retail Price Index; RPIX; Consumer Prices Index

1.8.1 Retail Prices Index (RPI)

The **Retail Prices Index (RPI)** is one of the key measures of inflation used in the UK economy. The RPI is calculated by looking at the prices of a basket of over 300 goods. The prices are then weighted to reflect the average household's consumption patterns. Important items, on which a high proportion of money is spent, are given higher weighting than peripheral items. Unlike the continental European measures of inflation, the RPI **includes mortgage interest payments** because the mortgage is an important element of expenditure for UK households. RPI also includes indirect taxes, e.g. alcohol and fuel duties and VAT.

The RPI is based on movements in prices from a base period – the current series runs from January 1987 (1987 = 100). The markets concentrate on the RPI figure since it is a good indicator of the level of inflation and, consequently, government reaction to it.

There is a measure that excludes mortgage interest payments from the RPI. This is known as **RPIX**, or the **underlying rate of inflation**.

1.8.2 Consumer Prices Index (CPI)

In November 2003, the **Consumer Prices Index (CPI)**, alternatively known as the Harmonised Index of Consumer Prices (HICP) was introduced in the UK. Harmonised indices are used throughout the European Union for the purposes of **international comparisons** of consumer price inflation, while the RPI remains the best indicator for consumer price inflation in the UK. The CPI and the RPI differ in the components included and methodology of calculation. For example, unlike the RPI, the CPI excludes mortgage interest payments as well as road fuel licence or tax, but will include an index for personal computers, whereas the RPI does not.

In addition to this, the CPI will look at the average household expenditure of the **entire UK population**. The RPI excludes expenditure of highest income households and pensioner households. Finally, whereas RPI is never revised, the CPI is a **revisable index**.

The CPI is used in economic policy making, as the basis for the UK's inflation target.

1.8.3 Impact of inflation

Inflation, in the broadest sense, is described as an increase in the general price index. At the time of writing, the CPI target set by the Chancellor was 2%, with this inflation target reviewed on an annual basis. Given this low level of inflation, the value of money halves every 35 years. If inflation were double this level (4%), the value of money would halve every eighteenth year while, with an inflation rate of 10%, it would halve in roughly 7.5 years.

It is extremely important to keep a check on the level of inflation. Inflation erodes the value of money, creating uncertainty for those investors and savers as to the value of their hard-earned cash in the future. The uncertainty element also comes into play when people attempt to budget for their future – with an inflationary environment, we don't know how much things will cost in later years.

Inequality is another problem that has to be addressed in an inflationary environment. Some members of the population, such as pensioners, retire on a fixed level of income and cannot therefore keep pace with increasing prices.

Finally, one might consider the impact of inflation on the international competitiveness of the UK. If domestic inflation exceeds that of our major trading partners, our goods and services are more expensive and, hence, far less desirable. In the longer term, this could have detrimental consequences for our manufacturing sector.

Equally, a negative rate of inflation – known as **deflation** – is also a risk. If prices are falling during an economic downturn, consumers may delay making purchases because they expect prices to fall further, and this can make a recession worse. Also, once it has started, deflation can be hard to stop: interest rate cuts that might encourage consumers to borrow and spend may not be possible because the rates may already be close to zero.

1.9 Economic measures

Learning objective **Know** the impact of the following economic data: Gross Domestic Product (GDP); Balance of Payments; Public Sector Net Cash Requirement (PSNCR): and level of unemployment

The government uses various measures to determine the health of the economy and its overall performance. An overview of some of the more important statistics you need to know about is given below.

1.9.1 Gross Domestic Product (GDP)

Gross Domestic Product (GDP) is the total value of output produced in the domestic economy, regardless of whom it belongs to. Therefore, US GDP would include the value of cars produced at a Japanese-owned car plant in the US, but would not include the value of produce made in the UK by American companies. GDP is a fairly precise measure of output within a country.

1.9.2 Balance of payments

The UK is an international economy that deals and transacts business around the world. The **balance of payments** account simply summarises this position in one statement, showing the inflows and outflows of the UK economy.

The flows are divided into two – the short-term flows (the **current account**) and the longer term transactions (the **capital account**).

The balance of payments current account includes the short-term flows into and out of the UK. Trade itself can be divided into two categories: **visible trade** and **invisible trade**.

Visible trade is trading conducted in physical goods. Over the past few decades, the UK has had a deficit on its visible trade balance with the rest of the world. In other words, the UK has imported more physical goods than it has exported. This situation would be impossible to maintain long term, were it not for the surplus the UK maintains on the invisible account.

Invisibles are trades in services and income flows. Invisible trade in the UK has been strong over the last 25 years or so. Included in the invisible earnings of the UK are the activities of the City of London, tourism and other services provided from the UK to overseas individuals. It is the surplus on the invisible trade which offsets the deficit the UK runs on visible trade and which, occasionally, results in a positive current account balance.

Also included within the invisible earnings of the UK are flows resulting from income on overseas investments, dividends and interest payments. The UK is one of the world's largest investors overseas, with particularly large stakes in the US.

Transactions in long-term capital flows are the longer term aspect of the balance of payments. Long-term investment flows either into or out of the UK. As noted above, this statement is referred to as the **capital account**.

It is impossible to give a general direction to the long-term flows. Much depends on the level of interest expressed by overseas investors in the UK and the opportunities to invest in the UK, which present themselves to UK investors, such as pension funds. These may, in the absence of a viable UK alternative, invest overseas. Obviously, one key determinant of the level of inward investment is the interest rate and, in particular, the real interest rate. When interest rates are high, they attract investment and thereby support the exchange rate through the balance of payments.

Overall, the balance of payments position is important economic data that is followed closely by the market. If the balance of payments current account is in deficit, i.e. where a country is importing more than it exports, eventually it must be corrected. One way of doing this is for its exchange rate to fall or devalue. At which point, imports become more expensive and exports become relatively cheap. This automatic mechanism should bring the balance of trade back into line. In reality, economic systems seldom work this efficiently, and the UK has maintained a deficit on the balance of trade, i.e. just visible. The statistics themselves, however, are notoriously unreliable, mainly due to the fact that they are based on a series of estimates.

1.9.3 Public sector net cash requirement

Every year the government tends to spend more money than it raises in tax and, somehow, it must fund the difference. This funding is achieved through the **Public Sector Net Cash Requirement (PSNCR)**. The requirement itself is either expressed as the set amount of money that is being raised by the government, or the percentage it represents of the Gross National Product. In the annual Budget, the Chancellor sets the PSNCR for the following year and it is then the responsibility of the Treasury's agency, the Debt Management Office, to issue gilts to achieve the majority of the required level of borrowing.

The market closely follows the PSNCR figure, since it indicates the amount of money the government is obliged to raise through the markets. This is important as it acts as a drain on funds. It also indicates how much control the government has over its levels of expenditure. If the PSNCR is growing too rapidly, it points to a government spending programme which is, perhaps, out of control.

1.9.4 Level of unemployment

The **rate of unemployment** is often used as an indicator of economic conditions. It is defined as the number of persons unemployed divided by the number of persons in the civilian labour force.

Formula to learn

$$\text{Level of unemployment} = \frac{\text{Number of persons unemployed}}{\text{Number of persons in civilian labour force}}$$

An unemployed person is defined as an individual who is not currently employed and is either actively seeking employment or waiting to begin a job or to return to work. People not actively seeking work, for whatever reason, are not treated as unemployed.

2 THE BANK OF ENGLAND

2.1 The functions of the Bank of England

Responsibility for banking supervision in the UK was transferred to the Financial Services Authority (FSA) as part of the Bank of England Act 1998. Although it lost responsibility for banking supervision, the Bank of England (the Bank) gained the freedom in May 1997 to set official UK interest rates. Interest rate decisions are taken by the Bank of England's **Monetary Policy Committee** (MPC).

The MPC is made up of representatives from the governing body of the Bank of England and industry experts, appointed by the Chancellor. The prime responsibility of the MPC is determining interest rates and meeting the target for overall inflation in the economy. The inflation target is set each year by the Chancellor of the Exchequer, not by the Bank. This is part of the Bank's responsibility to achieve price stability in the economy. The Bank implements interest rate decisions through its activities in the financial market, in particular, by setting the interest rate at which the Bank lends to other banks and financial institutions.

The Bank is also responsible for **maintaining stability in the financial system** by analysing and promoting initiatives to strengthen the financial system, and by monitoring financial developments to try to identify potential threats to financial stability. Consequently, the Bank is also known as the financial system's **'lender of last resort'**, providing funds in exceptional circumstances. In this work, the Bank co-operates closely with HM Treasury and the FSA.

The Bank of England can also intervene in the currency and money markets to:

- Maintain financial stability
- Provide the correct amount of notes and coins in circulation
- Provide statistical information used for analysis purposes
- Acts as banker to other banks to facilitate cheque clearing
- The Governor of the Bank of England may appoint the head of the Panel on Takeovers and Mergers

2.2 The functions of the Monetary Policy Committee

One of the main functions of the Monetary Policy Committee (MPC) is the setting of interest rates. Each month the MPC meets to discuss current trends in inflation and to decide on the direction and level of interest rates that will keep inflation within acceptable levels, given the Chancellor's inflationary target, which currently stands at **2%**, plus or minus 1% as measured by the CPI (also called the HCIP, as covered earlier. Inflation below the target of 2% is judged by the Bank of England to be just as bad as inflation above the target.

By raising **interest rates**, it is hoped that spending will be discouraged, thereby relieving inflationary pressures. Conversely, by lowering interest rates, it is hoped that more consumption will be encouraged which, in turn, will provide a boost to the economy.

3 FINANCIAL INSTITUTIONS

Learning objective   **Know** the role of the following within the financial services industry: retail banks; building societies; investment banks; pension funds; insurance companies; fund managers; stockbrokers; custodians; third party administrators (TPAs); industry trade and professional bodies

3.1 Introduction

The economy as a whole may be broken down into various **sectors** – such as finance, manufacturing and agriculture. The most important sector of the UK economy is the financial sector, reflecting London's status as one of the most important global financial centres. The activities of all the financial intermediaries combined total almost £1,000bn, or just under 30% of the economy.

3.2 Retail banks

The main function of **retail banks** used to be to take in deposits from individuals and provide current account and loan facilities. Retail banks have expanded their scope of business since the 1980s and now offer mortgages, life insurance, pensions and general investments (including share dealing facilities) in an attempt to provide their customers with a 'one-stop shopping' solution to all their financial needs. Internet and telephone banking facilities now complement the traditional branch network of all major retail banks.

BPP
LEARNING MEDIA

3.3 Investment banks

Investment banks act for the wholesale side of the market. They offer businesses the facility to raise finance and trade in various financial instruments.

Investment banks can also offer advisory services, which are used in the planning, or defence, of a takeover bid or strategic planning activities of various divisions of companies or the group as a whole.

3.4 Building societies

Building societies offer similar services to those of banks in the retail sector. However, their legal structure remains very different. Building societies are mutual societies owned by their members, who use their services. Since there are no shareholders and hence no dividend payout to consider, they should offer better savings and loan rates than the traditional banks. During the 1990s, many building societies changed their status to that of a bank, giving them more flexibility and the chance to access a wider range of financing.

3.5 Stockbrokers

Some of the functions undertaken by **stockbrokers** or securities houses overlap significantly with those services provided by investment banks. Below is a list of activities undertaken by securities houses. Some institutions will provide all these services, while others specialise in just one or two.

- **Broking** – dealing in shares on a client's behalf

- **Principal trading** – dealing in shares for the firm's account (also known as proprietary trading, or 'running a book')

- **Market making** – creating a liquid market by offering two-way (buying and selling) prices during normal market hours

- **Research and advice** – detailed analysis provided for retail and wholesale clients

- **Corporate finance** – the raising of finance or strategic planning which requires finance

- **Mergers and acquisitions** – advice on takeovers

- **Fund management** – investing other people's money according to a specific mandate

Inter-Dealer Brokers (IDBs) act as intermediaries between the various market makers. They provide a unique facility in the form of an anonymous dealing service, allowing market makers to unwind a particular position. In other words, they provide an advertising facility that only the market makers can access.

It should be noted, however, that the IDB does not take the position on its books – it undertakes **two matched principal to principal trades**. The IDBs make their money by charging a small commission to market makers who use them.

3.6 Pension funds

Although the State will pay out a basic pension, most individuals seek additional retirement funds through investing in **pension funds**. These may be provided by company initiatives (occupational pension schemes) or may be set up by the individual themselves (personal pensions).

Occupational pension schemes can be based on an employee's earnings at retirement and will then be linked to the number of years they have worked for the firm.

Contributions made to an approved pension scheme are eligible for tax relief – this applies both to contributions made by an employer and an employee, and also to contributions to a personal pension plan.

Pension fund managers must then select stocks from the various asset classes in order to meet the liabilities of the fund as people retire.

The National Association of Pension Funds (NAPF) is an industry body representing employer-sponsored pension funds.

3.7 Insurance companies

Insurance companies are often divided into general insurers and life insurers. The life insurance companies offer products that are designed to suit an individual's lifestyle needs, whereas general insurance (which may cover health, fire, car and pet insurance among others) is of a more fundamental nature. Time horizons of each tend to be different – life insurers have a long-term time horizon, while general insurers face payouts and must meet liabilities on a constant basis. This will affect their attitude towards risk and hence, their asset allocation and stock selection strategies. The insurance companies are represented by the Association of British Insurers (ABI).

3.8 Fund managers

Fund managers undertake investment activities on behalf of either individual customers or institutions. Fund managers must undertake a thorough assessment of the client's needs, whether a liability matching exercise is required or the maximisation of returns, prior to constructing and managing a portfolio. Naturally when a client wishes to have an individual tailor-made portfolio, the management charges will be relatively high to reflect the individual effort required. However, when individual investors pool their monies together with other investors in a collective investment arrangement, investors can not only take advantage of professional fund management services but also lower charges.

The fund management process involves managers analysing a wide range of asset classes, not only to match the needs of the clients but also to diversify away as much risk as possible.

3.9 Custodians

The role of **custodians** is to provide clients with custody (safekeeping), settlement and reporting services for all classes of financial instruments. Custodians are capable of looking after both registered and bearer style instruments but increasingly provide services in the processing of corporate actions.

Corporate actions will include benefit distributions such as dividend payments and ensuring that the correct number and type of shares are allocated to a client's account following a bonus issue or rights issue. Custodians also manage cash on behalf of investors, either moving cash for settlement or transferring surplus funds into interest-bearing accounts.

Withholding tax reclamation, where an investor has suffered withholding tax at source on overseas income, is another vital function performed by custodians. It is both expensive and time consuming for an individual investor to familiarise themselves with the complexities of a foreign country's taxation regime and thus far easier and efficient to have a custodian recover this tax on the client's behalf.

3.10 Third party administrators (TPAs)

Third party administrators provide outsourcing services to financial institutions. Essentially they act as the operations department and look after all aspects of the trade once the deal is struck. Thus, they provide settlement, reconciliation, custody and reporting services. They have grown in number over recent years because financial institutions have become more focussed on core activities and seek to avoid playing the 'technology game'. That is, they prefer not to continually invest in IT systems to keep pace with the ever changing demands of the financial services industry.

3.11 Industry trade and professional bodies

Industry trade bodies and **professional bodies** are associations that represent the interests of their members.

They may provide advice, training and networking opportunities.

Further, they may lobby the Government and other bodies to promote improvements and reform within the financial services industry.

In the financial sector, such bodies include the following.

- The **Association of British Insurers (ABI)** represents the collective interests of the UK's insurance industry. The Association lobbies on issues of common interest, participates in debates on public policy issues and acts as an advocate for high standards of customer service in the insurance industry. The ABI's 400 member companies provide around 90% of domestic insurance services sold in the UK.

- The **Association for Financial Markets in Europe (AFME)** represents the shared interests of a broad range of global and European participants in the wholesale financial markets. The London Investment Banking Association (LIBA) merged into the AFME on 1 November 2009.

- The **British Bankers Association (BBA)** is an association for the UK banking and financial services sector, speaking for 223 banking members from 60 countries on the range of UK or international banking issues and engaging with 37 associated professional firms.

- The **Association of Independent Financial Advisers (AIFA)** presents the collective view of its membership to the regulator and to policy makers who have an impact on the IFA market place and the business operation of IFAs.

- The **Chartered Institute for Securities & Investment** (CISI) is a London-based professional body for those who work in the financial and investment industry. The Institute's stated mission is: 'to set standards of professional excellence and integrity for the securities and investments industry, providing qualifications and promoting the highest level of competence to our members, other individuals and firms'.

- **CFA Institute** is a global, not-for-profit association of investment professionals that awards the Chartered Financial Analyst (CFA) designation. It promotes ethical standards and offers a range of educational opportunities online and around the world.

- The **International Capital Market Association (ICMA)** describes itself as s a self-regulatory organisation and a voice for the global capital market. The ICMA represents a range of capital market interests including global investment banks and smaller regional banks, as well as asset managers, exchanges, central banks, law firms and other professional advisers amongst its member firms. ICMA's market conventions and standards have been used in the international debt market for over 40 years.

- The **Investment Management Association (IMA)** is the trade body for the UK's asset management industry. Its members manage a variety of investment vehicles including authorised investment funds, pension funds and stocks and shares ISAs. The IMA's role is to represent the industry and to promote high standards.

- The **Tax Incentivised Savings Association (TISA)** is a trade association working with the retail financial services industry, political parties, HM Treasury, HM Revenue & Customs (HMRC) and the

Financial Services Authority to enhance and improve the range, features, benefits, promotion and quality of savings and investment schemes available in the UK.

4 THE LONDON STOCK EXCHANGE

Know the role of the following exchange: London Stock Exchange
Know the difference between the primary market and secondary market

4.1 The role of the London Stock Exchange

The **London Stock Exchange** (LSE) is, above all else, a business. Its primary objective is to establish and run a market place in securities. In any economy there are savers and borrowers. The exchange acts as a place in which they can meet.

Initially, the companies (the borrowers) issue shares to the investing public (the savers). This is known as the **primary market**. The main role of the LSE's primary market is to enable a company to issue shares. Investors would not be willing to invest their money unless they could see some way of releasing it in the future.

Consequently, the exchange must also offer a **secondary market** trading in second-hand shares, this allows the investor to convert the shares into cash.

Overview of the Exchange's activities

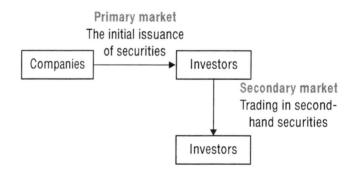

The primary market is the market for new issues of securities. The secondary market (markets in second-hand securities) exists to enable those investors who purchased investments to realise their investments into liquid cash. It is vital to ensure that the primary market is selective. A poor quality primary market will undermine the liquidity of the secondary market. Member firms of the LSE are active in the secondary market trading for their own firms (as **principal**) and/or on behalf of clients (as **agent**). This ability to act in both capacities is known as **dual capacity**.

4.2 Primary market

When new shares are to be issued to the general public, there are various marketing, financial and administrative considerations that need to be addressed. Companies wishing to issue shares often find it useful to hire the services of an issuing house or sponsor (usually these are services available from the investments banks), who will guide them through the process of preparing for the new issue and advertising the fact to potential new investors.

The next stage will involve receiving back the forms from potential investors, collating the information, making the allocations and finally preparing the share certificates for the successful applicants and rejection letters for the unsuccessful applicants along with their original cheques. We will consider two common methods for issuing shares into the primary market – **offer for sale** and **placing**, also known as **selective marketing**.

4.2.1 Offer for sale

Offer for sale

With an **offer for sale**, the company appoints an issuing house to deal with the public on its behalf. The issuing house advertises the security, obtains acceptances from the public, processes and allots shares and then sends the money to the company after the deduction of a fee. An offer for sale need not revolve around the issue of new securities; it can equally be used by a large shareholder selling a stake into the marketplace. The privatisations launched by the government over the last 20 years have been offers for sale, where a broking house has acted on the government's behalf to sell a large block of the shares in a company to the general public.

4.2.2 Placing (selective marketing)

By far the cheapest route available to a company for a new issue of shares is to opt for a placing. Under a placing, the company passes its shares to a particular broker, who then sells them to its client base. This removes most of the requirement for advertising, and is also the most efficient method of issuing shares. This method is also referred to as selective marketing, since the issue is only marketed to the clients of the sponsor – no one else would normally get to participate in this exercise. Some of the main advantages of this method are that it is cheap, fast and efficient, since all the clients are already known to the sponsor.

Placing

4.3 Secondary market

Investors would not be willing to invest their money in the primary market by buying shares unless they could see some way of releasing it in the future. Consequently, the exchange must also offer a **secondary market**, trading in second-hand shares. This allows the investor to convert the shares into cash, i.e. it gives liquidity. Thus, secondary trading takes place through an exchange, e.g. the LSE.

In order to ensure the stability of the secondary market, the exchange must establish strong controls over the companies that are allowed onto the market. Equally, the exchange must establish rules concerning the activities of brokers in the secondary market in order to preserve the reputation of the market. Many of these responsibilities have been passed onto the FSA in its role as the UK Listing Authority (UKLA). However, the LSE has itself a number of rules concerning the restriction on the investments in which a member firm can deal. These rules are designed to complement the UKLA rules.

Member firms of the LSE act in dual capacity, meaning that they can act either in an agency capacity to broke a client's business, or as principal and trade for the firm's own account. Some member firms take on additional responsibility and become market makers and provide continuity in prices of securities during normal market hours.

5 Derivatives and Commodity Markets

Know the characteristics of the derivatives and commodity markets: Trading (metals, energy)
Know the advantages and disadvantages of investing in the derivatives and commodity markets

5.1 NYSE Liffe

The most important London market for financial futures and options is the **London International Financial Futures and Options Exchange (Liffe)**, now known as **NYSE Liffe**.

NYSE Liffe is the global derivatives business of the **NYSE Euronext** group. In terms of financial products available, NYSE Liffe has both futures and options on individual equities, equity indices, e.g. FTSE 100, interest rate products and bond products. In addition to the range of financial derivatives available, Liffe also offers commodity derivatives on things like sugar, coffee and wheat.

5.2 Commodities

Commodities for investment purposes are essentially raw materials that can be bought and sold easily in large quantities on organised markets.

Commodities fall into one of two categories.

- **Hard commodities**: metals (gold, copper, lead, tin, nickel, uranium etc), diamonds, oil and gas
- **Soft commodities**: **agricultural** products including wool and cotton, and foodstuffs such as meats, cocoa, coffee, soya and sugar

There are both **spot markets** (where trades are conducted for immediate delivery) and **futures markets**, where prices can be agreed today for delivery at a later (predetermined) date.

Commodity futures may be traded on the following exchanges.

- **ICE Futures Europe®** – for the trading of energy derivative products, e.g. Brent Crude Oil

- **London Metal Exchange** (LME) – for the trading of base metal derivative products

- **Liffe** – for the trading of agricultural futures (such as wheat) and soft commodities (such as sugar, coffee and cocoa)

ICE Futures is part of **IntercontinentalExchange® (ICE)** of Atlanta, Georgia in June 2001. ICE is one of the world's largest electronic commodity and energy trading groups with particular emphasis upon the trading of OTC energy products.

5.3 Eurex

Eurex is one of the world's largest derivatives exchanges. In 2008, a total of 2.16 billion contracts were traded.

Eurex is a fully electronic exchange, created by Deutsche Börse AG and the Swiss Exchange in 1996. Its listed contracts are financial futures and options together with a range of equity options and index futures and options.

Trading on the fully computerised Eurex platform offers members technical access from any location, creating a global network. Members are linked to the Eurex system via a dedicated wide-area communications network (WAN). To facilitate access to Eurex outside of Switzerland and Germany, there are access points installed in Amsterdam, Chicago, New York, Helsinki, London, Madrid, Paris, Hong Kong, Sydney and Tokyo. Over 50% of all Eurex trades emanates from London.

5.4 Advantages and disadvantages

There are advantages and disadvantages of investing in derivatives and commodities markets.

Derivatives

Advantages

- A large value of an underlying asset can be controlled for a relatively low initial cost, potentially magnifying possible profits (an effect called 'gearing')

- An investor can gain exposure to the value of an asset without actually owning or taking delivery of the asset.

- A position can be taken which will profit if a price, such as a share price, falls.

Disadvantages

- The gearing effect magnifies potential losses as well as potential gains.

- There is a degree of 'liquidity risk': the risk that a derivative, particularly an 'over-the-counter' derivate (as opposed to an exchange-traded derivative) will be difficult to sell at the time the investor wishes to sell.

- For derivatives not protected by a clearing house system, there is the risk that the counterparty in the transaction may default.

Commodities

Advantages

- Exposure to commodities can serve to diversify a portfolio, as commodity values do not follow the values of other asset classes closely.

- Investments can be made in various ways, including through derivatives, commodity funds or commodity-producing companies, as well as through buying the actual commodity (e.g. gold).

Disadvantages

- Commodity prices are volatile, due to the economic cycle and other demand and supply factors, and so investments are risky.

- Agricultural commodities are highly susceptible to seasonal factors such as poor weather. Excess supply (a good harvest) can lead to prices falling substantially, while poor weather (e.g. frost in orange groves) can lead to losses.

6 WORLD SECURITIES MARKETS

arning objective | **Know** the characteristics of the following exchanges: New York Stock Exchange; NASDAQ; Euronext; Tokyo Stock Exchange and Deutsche Börse

6.1 Introduction

In today's market, investors seek to trade shares that are listed on foreign exchanges as well as exchanges such as the London Stock Exchange that are set up here in the UK. Below we discuss some of the popular overseas exchanges which investors based here in the UK use to access shares in foreign companies.

6.2 NYSE Euronext

The **New York Stock Exchange (NYSE)** traces its origins back more than 200 years and is today run by a president and board of 33 governors. Changes to its constitution in 2003 were aimed at increasing the level of transparency and reinforcing the concept of members' self-regulation. Shares and bonds, as well as a wide variety of other financial instruments, are available to America's 85 million investors, as well as investors internationally. The NYSE is one of the world's largest trading platforms in terms of the value of daily trades.

NYSE Euronext was formed in 2007 through the takeover of Euronext by the New York Stock Exchange. Euronext itself was formed in 2000 by the amalgamation of the Amsterdam, Brussels and Paris bourses, making it the second largest exchange in Europe behind the LSE. Euronext acquired Liffe in 2002 to become Euronext.liffe.

6.3 NASDAQ

The National Association of Securities Dealers Automatic Quote System (NASDAQ) was created in 1971 to be the world's first **electronic quote-driven stock market**. It specialised in providing a market for the more **innovative companies** and technology companies, against the more traditional backdrop of the NYSE (New York Stock Exchange). Today, NASDAQ is home to over 3,600 of the world's innovative companies, whose shares can be traded through a **sophisticated computer** and **telecommunications network**. This allows for an extremely liquid marketplace with a high degree of transparency, with all market participants able to see the same information on orders, quotations and spreads.

6.4 Deutsche Börse

Not only is the Deutsche Börse one of Europe's largest exchanges, but its Xetra US Stars trading system allows for the trading of US shares in Europe. Combining the trading hours of 09:00 to 20:00 (local time) with the support of at least five US market specialists, the Deutsche Börse provides a fast, efficient and reliable trading system for American shares outside the normal US market hours.

6.5 Stock exchanges in Japan

The Japanese market is served by five separate stock exchanges, of which the **Tokyo Stock Exchange (TSE)**, established in 1949, is perhaps the best known. In 1999, the TSE moved to **electronic trading** and by 2002 the TSE accounted for 92% of the value of all trades on the domestic Japanese exchanges. The TSE trades innovative derivative products, as well as Japanese stocks, and also provides settlement and clearing services and market information services.

7 FOREIGN EXCHANGE

Learning objective   Know the basic structure of the foreign exchange market including spot and forward rates.

7.1 Foreign exchange markets

Foreign exchange trading, or **FOREX** as it is commonly known, is the dealing by professional players of the currencies of various countries. The currency or FOREX market is the largest financial market in the world with a turnover in excess of $3,000bn each day, helped by its position between the two time zones of America and Asia. Let us now examine the two elements of the currency market, namely spot and forward, more closely. London is the biggest centre in the world for FOREX trading, with over 30% of the global market and over $1,000bn traded **per day**. Although some FOREX is required for overseas trade, the majority is for speculative purposes, where FOREX traders seek to exploit a particular view on interest rate differentials or exchange rate movements.

There is no formal market place for FOREX trades. Prices are advertised on screens and deals are conducted over telephones. The major players are the investment banks and specialist currency brokers. This is not a market place where the private investor gets involved directly – his currency needs are met through specialist money changing organisations, who themselves have accessed the currency markets through their own specialist broker.

FOREX transactions are described either as **spot** or **forward**. Spot means the trade is to meet immediate currency needs and will settle in two business days after the trade day (known as T + 2). Forward is when an exchange rate is agreed today for settlement at some future date, as agreed by the parties. This is a particularly useful way of eliminating risk from transactions requiring currency (import and export dealings) at some time in the future. Most currencies are quoted against the US dollar.

7.2 Spot transactions

The spot market is the market for immediate currency trades. These trades will settle in **two business days (T + 2)**. This may exclude public holidays in the countries of the two parties to the trade and also in the country of the currency. For example, a German bank dealing in the sterling market with an American bank would have to take into account public holidays in Germany, the US and the UK.

The spot market quotes bid offer prices in the form of a spread, normally based against the value of one US dollar. The main exception to this is £\$ where the $ is quoted against the value of one pound (the sterling / dollar rate being known as **cable**).

£\$ spot exchange rate

$1.4625 – $1.4635

The buyer's rate   The seller's rate

£1 will get $1.4625 $1.4635 will get £1

To help you remember which is the correct rate to use, it may be useful to remember that the bank will always give you the worst of the two rates. When selling you dollars, they will only give you $1.4625 instead of $1.4635. When buying dollars from you, they will give you £1 for each $1.4635 you give them, rather than $1.4625.

7.3 Forward transactions

The forward market is a market in currencies at an agreed date in the future. It enables you to agree a rate today (the forward rate) at which the currencies will be exchanged on the agreed future date. The benefit of this is certainty – although you do not need the foreign currency until three months' time, you can fix an exchange rate today.

One point about this market is that it does not reflect expectations of what spot rates will be in three, six or nine months' time. Forward rates reflect spot rates now adjusted for the difference in interest rates over the period concerned in the two countries or currency areas.

8 RETAIL AND PROFESSIONAL BUSINESS

Know the function of and difference between retail and professional business and who the main customers are in each case: retail clients and professional clients

8.1 The retail market

The retail market is aimed at individuals, called retail clients. These individuals range from high net worth (possibly sophisticated) investors right through to small investors. Firms in the retail sector might provide discretionary, advisory or execution-only services to individual retail clients but ultimately the buyers of financial products are individuals. These products range from shares, bonds, derivatives, insurance, pensions, ISAs and units in collective investment schemes.

8.2 The professional market

The professional or wholesale market is aimed at financial institutions. These institutions include investment banks, securities houses, insurance companies, fund managers, pension suppliers, charities and local authorities. While many of these organisations will have underlying clients, it is the trading conducted between these institutions that is referred to as wholesale business.

9 INVESTMENT DISTRIBUTION CHANNELS

Know the role of the following investment distribution channels: Independent Financial Adviser; tied adviser, platforms and execution only

9.1 Independent financial advisers

Independent Financial Advisers (IFAs) may advise on products from a range of companies across the market, or across a range of several product providers.

IFAs give advice on investments, savings plans, pensions, mortgages or insurance. Some advisers specialise in one type of product while others give general advice about all areas.

9.2 Tied advisers

Tied advisers provide a similar service to IFAs but they usually work for a bank, building society or insurance company and only offer that company's products.

9.3 Platforms

A company which trades securities or currencies is sometimes referred to as offering a trading **platform**.

For the professional market, in addition to the traditional exchanges such as the London Stock Exchange, liberalised rules under MiFID have led to the creation of a new generation of trading platforms called '**multilateral trading facilities**' (**MTFs**). MTFs bring together multiple buyers and sellers in financial instruments and match client orders in a similar to way to the traditional exchanges.

MTFs, such as Turquoise (now part of London Stock Exchange Group) and Chi-X, offer the prospect of firms making use of what are called **dark liquidity pools**, whereby firms can buy and sell blocks of shares off-exchange, away from the public domain. This offers trading anonymity, without prices being displayed on the public order book usually found on exchanges.

9.4 Execution only

Where a broker provides dealing services only, without providing any advice to the client, this form of business is called '**execution only**'. The nature of the service provided must be made clear to the client.

CHAPTER ROUNDUP

- The economy can be analysed using a circular flow model. A 'mixed economy' such as that of the UK allows market forces to determine outcomes, with some State intervention.

- Credit creation by the commercial banks is a part of the process of expansion of the money supply.

- Inflation creates problems, and the Bank of England aims to control the inflation rate when it sets the interest rates.

- The Bank of England is the UK's central bank, with responsibilities in maintaining the stability of the financial system, and a role as the lender of last resort.

- The task of setting short-term interest rates is the responsibility of the Bank's independent Monetary Policy Committee.

- Key financial institutions include the retail ('High Street') banks and building societies, investment banks, stock broking firms, insurance companies, pension funds and fund managers.

- The London Stock Exchange (LSE) acts as both a primary market, in which companies can raise new finance by offering new securities, and a secondary market, in which securities can be sold to new investors.

- Other markets include Euronext.liffe for financial futures and options, and the commodities markets.

- UK investors can also make use of stock exchanges around the world.

- Currency (FOREX) trading can be conducted spot for immediate needs, or forward, fixing a rate for future settlement.

- The financial sector encompasses retail business with individuals and professional business with institutional clients.

TEST YOUR KNOWLEDGE

Check your knowledge of the Chapter here, without referring back to the text.

1. In the circular flow model of the economy, the value produced by firms is returned to households as
    .... In this model, 0............ = E............... = I............... . *[Fill in the blanks]*

2. The 'Euro zone' is *best* described as an area in which:

    A   Exchange rates between member countries are floating

    B   Exchange rates between member countries are pegged to each other

    C   There is a monetary union, with the exchange rate being allowed to float

    D   There is a monetary union, with the exchange rate being pegged to a trade-weighted basket of
         currencies

3. The UK Government's inflation target is based on:

    A   RPI
    B   RPIX
    C   RPIY
    D   CPI

4. Which country's GDP includes the value of a Toyota car engine produced in the UK?

5. In what area of international trade is the UK particularly strong, especially in view of the activities in the
    City of London?

6. What is the term describing the Government's funding shortfall?

7. What type of market participant 'creates a liquid market by offering two-way (buying and selling) prices
    during normal market hours'?

8. A rate agreed today for an exchange of currencies at a future date is called a .... rate.

    A rate agreed today for an exchange of currencies now is called a .... rate. *[Fill in the blanks]*

9. What does 'cable' refer to in currency trading?

TEST YOUR KNOWLEDGE: ANSWERS

1. In the circular flow model of the economy, the value produced by firms is returned to households as *income*. In this model, *Output = Expenditure = Income*.

   See Section 1.1

2. The correct answer is C. The euro effectively floats in the currency markets.

   See Section 1.6

3. D is the correct answer. The Consumer Prices Index (CPI) is also known as the Harmonised Index of Consumer Prices

   See Section 1.8.2

4. The value of the production of the engine is included in the domestic economy's GDP, i. e. the UK's GDP.

   See Section 1.9.1

5. The UK's trade performance in services ('invisibles') is particularly strong, and the City of London contributes greatly to this.

   See Section 1.9.2

6. Public Sector Net Cash Requirement.

   See Section 1.9.3

7. Market makers.

   See Section 3.5

8. A rate agreed today for an exchange of currencies at a future date is called a forward rate.

   A rate agreed today for an exchange of currencies now is called a spot rate.

   See Sections 7.2 and 7.3

9. The US dollar/sterling exchange rate.

   See Section 7.2

2

Asset Classes

The limited company structure is fundamental to the markets for capital in a developed economy. We need to understand the benefits and risks of owning shares in a company. We need to know the types of corporate action that a company can put into effect.

Public companies may have a full Stock Exchange listing, or there is the Alternative Investment Market for smaller companies.

While shares ('equities') make up one asset class, 'fixed interest' securities or 'bonds' are another.

Finally in this chapter we will outline the workings of the money markets, on which shorter term instruments are traded.

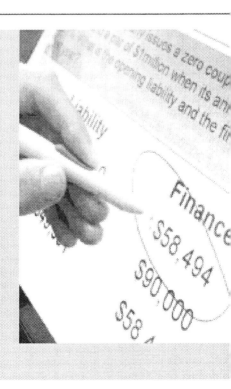

CHAPTER CONTENTS

		Page
1	The Companies Act	28
2	Share Ownership	31
3	Corporate Actions	33
4	Listing Status	36
5	The Alternative Investment Market (AIM)	38
6	Indices	38
7	SETS	39
8	SETSqx and SEAQ	42
9	Euroclear UK & Ireland: CREST	43
10	UK Government Bonds	46
11	Other Fixed Interest Securities	49
12	Money Market Instruments	53
	Chapter Roundup	55
	Test Your Knowledge	57

CHAPTER LEARNING OBJECTIVES

Money Market Instruments

- **Know** the difference between a capital market instrument and a money market instrument

- **Know** the definition and features of the following

  - Treasury Bill
  - Commercial Paper
  - Certificate of Deposit

- **Know** the advantages and disadvantages of investing in money market instruments

World Stock Markets

- **Know** the types and uses of a stock exchange index

- **Know** the differences between the following London Stock Exchange indices

  - FTSE 100
  - FTSE 250
  - FTSE 350
  - FTSE All Share

- **Know** to which market the following indices relate

  - Dow Jones Industrial Average
  - S&P 500
  - Nikkei 225
  - CAC40
  - XETRA Dax
  - NASDAQ Composite

Equities

- **Know** how a company is formed and the differences between private and public companies

- **Know** the features and benefits of ordinary and preference shares

  - Dividend
  - Capital gain
  - Share benefits
  - Right to subscribe for new shares
  - Right to vote

- **Understand** the risks associated with owning shares

  - Price risk
  - Liquidity risk
  - Issuer risk

- **Know** the definition of a corporate action and the difference between mandatory, voluntary and mandatory with options

- **Understand** the following terms

  - Bonus/scrip/capitalisation issues
  - Rights issues
  - Dividend payments
  - Takeover/merger

- **Know** the purpose and format of Annual General Meetings

- **Know** the main requirements for listing on the London Stock Exchange

- **Know** the role of the Alternative Investment Market (AIM)

- **Know** how shares are traded on the London Stock Exchange – SETS/SEAQ/SETSqx

- **Know** the method of holding title – registered v bearer

- **Understand** the role played by Euroclear UK & Ireland in the clearing and settlement of equity trades

  - Uncertificated transfers
  - Participants (members, payment banks, registrars)

- **Know** the advantages and disadvantages of a company obtaining a listing of its shares on the London Stock Exchange

Government Bonds

- **Know** the definition and features of UK government bonds

  - DMO maturity classifications
  - How they are issued

Corporate Bonds

- **Know** the definitions and features of the following types of bond

  - Domestic
  - Foreign
  - Eurobond
  - Asset-backed securities
  - Zero-coupon
  - Convertible

Bonds

- **Know** the advantages and disadvantages of investing in different types of bonds

- **Be able to calculate** the flat yield of a bond

- **Understand** the role of credit rating agencies and the differences between investment and non-investment grades

1 THE COMPANIES ACT

1.1 Background

Companies legislation is designed to achieve a number of ends. In particular, it attempts to protect shareholders from abuses of power by the directors and to protect the general public from the abuse of limited liability.

The **Companies Act 2006 (CA 2006)** has repealed almost all of the previous Companies Acts, and re-states the law in plainer English.

1.2 Formation of a company

Learning objective	**Know** how a company is formed and the differences between private and public companies

A company is formed when capital is provided, by perhaps a small group of investors, for the creation of a separate entity to undertake particular business activities.

Companies may either be **private companies** (their name appears with the abbreviation 'Ltd'), in which case they cannot offer shares to the general public, or **public companies** (their name has the abbreviation 'plc' after it), which allows them to issue shares to the general public.

The legal nature of a company has at its core the concept of **limited liability**, which means that the providers of share capital are limited in terms of loss to the initial amount they contributed in order to buy shares.

Each company must have two constitutional documents.

1.2.1 The Memorandum of Association

The **Memorandum of Association** is the **external** rulebook of the company governing its relationship with the outside world.

The Memorandum must state

- The company's name
- The location of the company's registered office (England and Wales or Scotland)
- That the company's liability is limited
- If the company is to be a public limited company (plc)
- The share capital of the company
- The objectives of the company, in other words, the main trading objectives of the company

1.2.2 The Articles of Association

The **Articles of Association** are the **internal** rulebook of the company governing the relationship between the company and its members (shareholders). There are standard terms contained within the Act in **Table A**. However, each company can create its own rules.

Once established, the provisions are binding on the shareholders in their relationships with the company and with each other. Copies of these documents are kept by the **Registrar of Companies** at Companies House in Cardiff or Edinburgh.

1.3 Company meetings and resolutions

Know the purpose and format of Annual General Meetings

A company must hold an **Annual General Meeting (AGM)** every calendar year, although there can be a maximum of 15 months between each meeting.

21 calendar days' notice must be given prior to this meeting, although this notice period may be waived if **all** (100%) of the shareholders agree.

The AGM will at least consider the following.

- Approving the accounts
- Appointing or removing directors
- Appointing auditors and giving power to the directors to fix their remuneration

If any other meeting needs to be called during the year, in order to obtain specific approval for an event, this is termed an **Extraordinary General Meeting (EGM)**.

- Following implementation of the EU Shareholder Rights Directive, the general position is that **21 calendar days' notice** is required for an EGM.

- However, traded (listed) companies may require a minimum of **14 days'** notice, provided that they pass a **special resolution** annually and offer all shareholders the ability to appoint proxies electronically.

There are a number of detailed rules within the CA 2006 Act concerning the appointment of the Chairman of the meeting and quorum. In general, a quorum is achieved when two members are present.

1.4 Shareholders' ability to vote

Know the features and benefits of ordinary and preference shares: dividend; capital gain; share benefits; right to subscribe for new shares; right to vote

The shareholders of a company are the **owners** of the company. There are a number of key events and decisions which can only be taken by the shareholders, and these decisions are taken in a general meeting. If a shareholder is unable to attend the meeting in order to cast their vote in person, they are able to appoint a **proxy** or ask the Chairman to vote on their behalf.

1.5 Ordinary shares

Ordinary shares are often referred to as **equity shares**. The term 'equity' means that each share has an equal right to share in profits. For example, if a company has 10,000 ordinary shares, each share is entitled to $1/10,000$ of the profits made during any period.

The rights of ordinary shares are detailed in the company's constitutional documents and in particular, the **Articles of Association**. However, it is normal for ordinary shares to possess a **vote**. This means that the holder of any ordinary shares may attend and vote at any meetings held by the company. Whilst the day-to-day control of the company is passed into the hands of the directors and managers, the shareholders must have the right to decide upon the most important issues that affect the business.

1.6 Preference shares

Another type of share which a company can issue is a **preference share** which takes on debt-like characteristics and offers only limited risks and returns.

A preference share is preferred in two basic forms.

1. The preference share **dividend must be paid out before any ordinary dividend can be paid**. It is conventional for preference shares to be **cumulative** and if the dividend is not paid in any one year, the arrears and the current year's dividend must be paid before any ordinary dividend can be paid in the future. The assumption is that preference shares are cumulative unless otherwise stated.

2. The second form of preference is in the order of payout upon the winding up of a company. **Preference shares will be paid prior to ordinary shares, on liquidation, up to the nominal value of the shares**. Equity shares would receive anything that remains after **all other** investors have been paid.

Offsetting these benefits, preference shareholders do have to give up a number of rights normally attached to shares. Firstly, the dividend on preference shares is normally a **fixed dividend** expressed as a percentage of the nominal value. For example, 7% £1 NV preference shares – these shares would pay a dividend each year of 7p per share.

Secondly, it is conventional for preference shares not to carry **voting rights**. However, most company constitutions contain a clause that states that if the dividend on a cumulative preference share has not been paid for **five years**, preference shareholders will receive the right to attend and vote at general meetings of the company. It should be remembered that, as with all dividends, the payment is at the discretion of the company and no shareholder may sue for a dividend.

1.7 Overview

One of the key maxims of investment is **greater risk requires greater potential reward**. There are various types of asset classes or securities available for investment purposes, each with a unique risk and reward profile.

For an investor wishing to become a part owner in a company and potentially receive an income distribution in the form of dividends, as well as capital growth from an increase in the share price, the purchase of shares or equities is ideal.

In much the same way that governments finance their deficits through the use of debt, companies who wish to spend more than they currently have available may also borrow money through the issuance of bonds. Due to the increased risk of default, these bonds will yield more than government debt.

For investors seeking a guaranteed regular income payment, along with the expectation of receiving back the original amount of their loan, investments in gilts (UK government loan stock) or other fixed income products would be more suitable.

2 SHARE OWNERSHIP

Understand the risks associated with owning shares: price risk; liquidity risk; issuer risk
Know the method of holding title – registered v bearer

2.1 Rights and benefits of share ownership

Ordinary shareholders' voting rights, and the main reasons for owning a share, are considered below. Generally speaking, investors hope to be able to buy shares at a fairly low price, hold the shares for a period of time before selling them at a higher price and netting a profit.

- When an investor believes the price of a share or the market as a whole will rise, he is said to be **bullish**. A **bull** will thus buy shares now, believing he will be able to sell out at a profit later, when indeed the shares have risen in price.

- Conversely, an investor who believes that a share's price or the market as a whole will fall, will seek to sell his shares now before the price does indeed move down. These investors are said to be **bears**, i.e. they possess a **bearish** viewpoint.

2.1.1 Voting rights

As far as decision-making within the company is concerned, there are a number of key events and decisions which can only be taken by the shareholders. These decisions are normally taken at the Annual General Meeting (AGM). If a shareholder is unable to attend, then he is able to appoint a **proxy** or ask the Chairman to vote on his behalf.

The AGM will at least consider:

- Receiving and approving the accounts for the financial year
- Appointing or removing directors
- Appointing or removing auditors and giving power to the directors to fix their remuneration
- Approve the dividend proposed by the directors

2.1.2 Dividends

Many investors purchase shares because of the attraction of a stream of **income**. While it must be remembered that companies legally do not have to declare a **dividend**, many of them do in order to maintain shareholder loyalty. Companies may pay an interim dividend based on the six-month results, and declare a final dividend based on the year-end results. This will not be paid until the shareholders have agreed it at the AGM.

A company will normally close the register (books close date) on a Friday. With standard settlement of T + 3, this means an investor will need to trade by Tuesday of that week to trade cum div (with the right to receive the next dividend).

Therefore, the share will start to trade ex-div (without the dividend) from the Wednesday.

Some companies give their shareholders the choice to take their dividend in new shares, rather than cash. New shares are created, but in a way that there will be no significant impact on the share price. The investors are taxed as if they had taken the cash dividend.

2.1.3 Capital growth

Not only do shares offer income in the form of dividends, they also offer the possibility of capital growth when the share price rises, usually over the longer term.

2.1.4 Other perks

Shareholders who hold their shares in their own name rather than in a nominee account may receive additional benefits (or 'perks') from the company in which they hold shares. These may include discounts on the firm's products or free gifts of the company's products.

2.1.5 Right to subscribe for new shares

Under the Companies Act, companies have an obligation to ensure that any new shares issued for cash are first offered to existing shareholders, in proportion to their existing shareholdings. However, shareholders may disapply their pre-emptive rights through a special resolution. We will discuss the mechanics of **rights issues** later in this chapter.

2.2 Risks of owning shares

While there are many potential benefits that come with owning shares as outlined above, there are also associated risks.

There are many forms of risk but two of the most common risk categories are **market risk** and **credit risk**.

- **Market risk** is defined as the risk of loss of earnings or capital arising from changes in the value of financial instruments and has itself a number of underlying components of which price level risk and liquidity risk are perhaps the biggest elements.

  - **Price risk** is the primary source of market risk and arises due to **adverse changes in the price** of the share (or other financial instrument). The share price may be affected by fluctuating exchange rates and changes in interest rates too.

  - **Liquidity risk** is the risk associated with not being able to buy or sell shares in a market or obtain **proper pricing**, for example when there is a shortage of market makers for that particular share.

- **Credit risk** is the risk of loss arising from the **failure of a counterparty** to pay its obligations. Within this category, counterparty risk, settlement risk and issuer risk all contribute to credit risk.

  - **Issuer risk** is the risk of **default** when one institution holds debt securities issued by another company, which then defaults on its obligation to pay.

2.3 Methods of holding title

In the UK, all shares are issued in **registered form**, which means that the company has a register that contains the details of all shareholders. The share register is normally maintained by the company registrar.

2.3.1 Physical mechanics

Most trading of shares is done through the LSE and settlement takes place through CREST, which is operated by Euroclear UK & Ireland. The advantage of using the LSE is that it provides a focus for liquidity and has certain rules governing the conduct of trades and transactions.

Where shares are transferred outside the LSE, individuals will agree a price and then exchange cash against document, delivery versus payment (DVP). However, the purchaser must have their name entered in the register of shareholders. This is executed via a legal transfer document which is signed by the original owner.

Summary

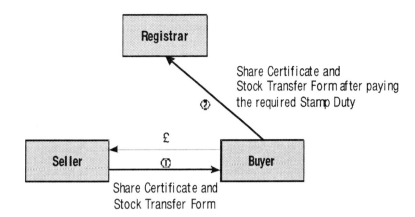

2.3.2 Legal documentation

In order to transfer the ownership of a registered share a legal transfer document is required, the **Stock Transfer Form (STF)**. The STF details the nature of the security, certifies ownership, and then transfers that ownership to the person or persons named as transferee.

Before the registrar can register the transfer, it needs to be shown that **stamp duty** has been paid on the transaction so the purchaser must send the completed stock transfer form, with the appropriate fee for the stamp duty, to the local HMRC office, which stamps the certificate.

Once the registrar receives the share certificate and the signed and stamped transfer document, ownership is then transferred on to the register. It is from this date that the benefits of ownership passes to the new owner of the shares. As proof of entry on to the register, the new owner receives a new share certificate, showing the correct name.

Gilt-edged securities are the outstanding debt obligations of the Government. As with UK equities, gilts are issued in **registered form**. The register is maintained jointly by the Debt Management Office (DMO) and Computershare Investor Services plc.

However, some securities are issued in **bearer form**. An example of a bearer security would be a Eurobond, where there is no formal register of ownership held by the Eurobond issuer.

3 CORPORATE ACTIONS

ming objectives | **Know** the definition of a corporate action and the difference between mandatory, voluntary and mandatory with options
Understand the following terms: bonus/scrip/capitalisation issues; rights issues; dividend payments; takeover/merger

3.1 Types of corporate action

Corporate actions are interactions between a company and its shareholders. These may relate to the payment of a dividend, corporate circulars relating to forthcoming meetings such as an Annual General Meeting or Extraordinary General Meeting, the subsequent issue of shares through either a bonus or a rights issue, or decisions regarding takeovers.

Corporate actions fall into three categories.

- Mandatory
- Voluntary (optional)
- Mandatory with options

Mandatory corporate actions take place regardless of investor participation. Examples of mandatory events are **dividend payments** and **bonus issues**, where the dividend will be paid or new shares issued without shareholders making a decision on the event.

A **voluntary** (or optional) corporate action is an event that will only occur upon election of the shareholder within a limited period of validity. The shareholder must inform the company of their choice. An example of a voluntary event would be a **takeover**.

Finally, a **mandatory event with options** is one where an event will occur, but the shareholder decides on how he or she will participate. An example of this type of corporate action would be a **rights issue**, where the company will issue new shares at a stipulated subscription price, but an investor may elect whether or not to participate and how they will participate.

3.2 Bonus issues

Bonus issues are also referred to as **scrip issues, capitalisation issues**, cap issues and free issues. Here, the company issues new shares to its existing shareholders but does not require a payment for them from the shareholder. The main reason for bonus issues is to dilute the price of the share in the market place by spreading it over a larger number of securities. This is felt to be important in the UK markets since shares with too high a value may discourage activity, and therefore liquidity, in a stock.

A bonus issue will theoretically cause the share price of the company to fall.

Example: Bonus issues

A company undertakes a 1 for 4 bonus issue, i.e. for every four shares currently in issue, one new share is issued. (Note that in the US this would be referred to as a **5 for 4**.) The company's share price prior to the bonus issue was £3.00 (this may be referred to as the **cum bonus** or **cum cap** share price). What is the theoretical impact of the bonus issue on the company's share price?

Solution

To establish the theoretical impact on the share price, we need to consider the total value of the shares and the number of shares this value is spread over, as follows.

	No. of Shares	Price per Share (£)	Total Value (£)
Before the bonus issue	4	3.00	12.00
Issue of one bonus share	1	Free	–
After the bonus issue	5		12.00

Hence, the theoretical share price after the issue is £2.40 (£12.00 ÷ 5 shares). It may be a little higher in practice if it improves the marketability of the shares.

Exam tip | In the exam, you will not be required to calculate the theoretical share price after the bonus issue.

3.3 Rights issue

Companies have an obligation under the Companies Act to ensure that any new shares issued for cash are first offered to existing shareholders (the right of first refusal or **pre-emption rights**), through what is known as a **rights issue**.

Example: Rights issues

A 1 for 3 rights issue is made at a price of £4.00 (the **subscription price**) when the current market price is £5.00 (the **cum rights price**).

A rights letter will be despatched to each shareholder telling them of their right to subscribe for a certain number of shares. For example, a shareholder who currently owns 3,000 shares will receive a letter telling him of his right to subscribe for 1,000 new shares at a price of £4.00 each.

The rights letter will be despatched to all shareholders who are on the register of shareholders on the particular date set by the company, referred to as the **on register** day.

What options are available to the shareholder?

Solution

Once the rights letter has been despatched the shareholder then has four courses of action from which to choose.

1. To take up the shares (at £4 each) and hold them.

2. To take up the shares (at £4 each) and sell them, i.e. sell them at the ex-rights price to realise the surplus over the subscription price.

3. To sell the rights nil paid, i.e. to realise the surplus over the subscription price (see below).

4. To do nothing, allow the rights to expire and the company will then sell the shares in the market place. Any surplus over the subscription price less administration costs – in this case £4.00 – will then be despatched to the shareholder.

3.4 Valuation of a rights issue

3.4.1 Theoretical ex-rights prices

It is important to be able to determine the amount the rights nil paid can be sold for.

The first step is to calculate the value of a share after the rights issue – the **theoretical ex-rights price**.

Example: Theoretical ex-rights price

1 for 3 rights issue @ £4.00 when market price (or **cum rights price**) is £5.00.

	No. of Shares	Price per Share (£)	Total Value (£)
Existing holding	3	5.00	15.00
Exercise right to buy	1	4.00	4.00
After the rights issue	4		19.00

As a result of the rights issue, the shareholder has four indistinguishable (fungible) shares with a total value of £19.00.

Therefore, each share now has a value of $\dfrac{£19}{4}$ = **£ 4.75**

As a result of the rights issue, the share price will, theoretically, fall from its current market level of £5.00 to £4.75, referred to as the theoretical ex-rights price. This reflects the dilution aspect of issuing one new share at £4.00 when the existing market price of shares is £5.00.

Exam tip	In the exam, you will not be required to calculate the theoretical ex-rights price or nil paid rights value.

3.4.2 Nil paid values

If the new share price is £4.75, then the maximum price that anybody would be prepared to pay for the unpaid rights, which gives the right to buy the shares at £4.00, would be **75p**. Anything more than that, and buyers may as well go into the market and buy the shares after the rights issue.

Formula to learn	Nil paid rights value = Ex-rights price - Subscription price

We are dealing here with the hypothetical situation. In reality, prices might reflect a number of other factors, and might rise or fall by different amounts.

3.4.3 Underwriting

During a rights issue, the issuing company may approach a third party to act as **underwriter**. In the event that any shares remain unsold, the underwriter will be obliged to purchase these shares. This means that the issuing company is assured a specific amount of cash.

3.5 Takeovers and mergers

The term '**takeover**' relates to a situation where one company acquires the share capital of another company. This results in a change of ownership and control.

Mergers run along a similar theme with two companies agreeing to combine their operations and share capital and create a new entity.

4 LISTING STATUS

Learning objectives	**Know** the main requirements for listing on the London Stock Exchange. **Know** the advantages and disadvantages of a company obtaining a listing of its shares on the London Stock Exchange.

The FSA grants the LSE the status of Recognised Investment Exchange. The FSA in its role as the **UK Listing Authority (UKLA)** also decides which companies' securities may be listed on the LSE (a statutory role known as the **Competent Authority**).

The LSE operates two levels of entry into the market, namely the **Full List** and the **Alternative Investment Market (AIM)**. Of the two, the full list is the senior market, and membership demands the most onerous responsibilities. Eligibility to join the Full List is determined by the UKLA, whilst admission to AIM is determined under the LSE's AIM Rules.

BPP
LEARNING MEDIA

4.1 Advantages of listing

Perhaps the most important advantage of listing is the opportunity to **raise funds** for the future growth and development of a company. A listing gives a company access to major investors on a worldwide basis. There is also a certain amount of **prestige** that is associated with being a listed company – rather like the idea of becoming a member of an exclusive club. When shares are listed, it gives a company that has launched a takeover bid an added element of flexibility, in that it may offer (either in part or in full) its own shares as consideration for the shares of the target company.

4.2 Disadvantages of listing

There are, however, some disadvantages that a company would have to consider prior to beginning the process of seeking a listing. Since a company's shares are freely tradeable, it would be possible for another company to build up a significantly large position that it could use as a platform from which to launch a takeover bid.

When shares are held by large institutional investors, there is the risk that they could lobby management of a company for a particular outcome, in other words, the founding members and directors **lose control** and autonomy. At the same time, market volatility and negative sentiment within the marketplace could have a detrimental effect on the company's share price, thus creating problems for a company that is fundamentally sound.

Finally, there are **costs** associated with being a listed company – for example, initial listing fees, advisory fees and annual membership fees that must be paid to the exchange on which the company's shares trade. Listed companies must also realise that being in the public domain brings with it a certain element of publicity – a fickle press can be extremely harmful to a company, whilst a positive press report adds much gloss to a company's profile.

4.3 Listing requirements

The UKLA rules for admission are contained in the Listing Rules. These detail the requirements a company must meet prior to being admitted to the full list.

From 6 April 2010, there are two tiers of listing: **Premium** and **Standard**. To become part of the FTSE UK index series, a company must have a Premium listing, which requires a standard exceeding the European benchmark requirements.

The following conditions in the Listing Rules must be met for a Premium listing.

- The company must be a plc.
- The expected market value of **shares** issued by the company must be at least **£700,000**.
- All securities issued must be freely transferable.
- The company must have a trading record of at least **three years**.
- The shares must be sufficiently **marketable**, and **25%** of the company's capital being available for public purchase (known as the **free float**) is seen to satisfy this requirement.
- All applicants for membership agree to be bound by the **continuing obligations** of the Listing Rules. These obligations require the company to:
    - Notify the LSE of any price-sensitive information
    - Publish information about significant transactions undertaken by the company
    - Inform the LSE of any changes in the important registers of ownership of the shares, such as material and notifiable interests and directors' shareholdings
    - Notify the LSE of dividends

–   Issue reports. Annual financial statements must be available within six months of the year end, and in addition, LSE companies are obliged to produce half-yearly results within 90 calendar days of the half year.

All of the above obligations would be made through one of the official **Regulatory Information Service (RIS)** providers approved by the UKLA.

The UKLA has the power o require a company seeking a listing to appoint a **sponsor** in certain circumstances, to advise the company on their obligations. Often the sponsor will already be involved in a transaction as financial adviser, and is expected to provide an effective challenge to forecasts and statements made by the company.

A **Standard** listing is most likely to appeal to a company that does not meet the requirements of a three year track record, appointment of a sponsor and more extensive continuing obligations. However, there is arguably little difference between the Standard listing requirements and those of the Alternative Investment Market (AIM).

5   THE ALTERNATIVE INVESTMENT MARKET (AIM)

Learning objective	**Know** the role of the Alternative Investment Market (AIM)

In 1995, the London Stock Exchange introduced the **Alternative Investment Market (AIM)**. This forum for trading a company's shares has enabled companies to have their shares traded through the LSE in a lightly regulated regime. Smaller companies can obtain access to the market through the AIM, at a lower cost and regulatory burden, and without needing a three-year track record, for example.

6   INDICES

Learning objectives	**Know** the types and uses of a stock exchange index **Know** the differences between the following London Stock Exchange indices: FTSE 100; FTSE 250; FTSE 350 and FTSE All Share

6.1 Introduction

An **index** measures the movement in a particular market over time, starting with a base, normally 100, and showing movements from a certain date onwards. This allows investors to see at a glance what is happening to that sector in general.

Share price indices come in a variety of forms depending on the use to which the market puts them. One important difference between **indices** is whether they are based on a weighted or an unweighted index. A weighted index gives more value to the largest shares within the pool. For example, the FTSE 100 Index is based on the top 100 shares in the UK market. However, this is weighted and, therefore, the largest shares are a bigger part of the index.

The FTSE 100 index weighting is adjusted to take into account each share's **free float**. Essentially, this makes the weighting reflect the proportion of a company's shares that are freely available to trade, for example shares retained by the government following a privatisation would not normally be included in the free float.

On the other hand, the Dow Jones Index in the US is an unweighted index and therefore, price movements on each of the 30 shares that make up the index make an equal impact on the overall index number.

6.2 The use of indices

Know to which market the following indices relate: Dow Jones Industrial Average; S&P 500; Nikkei 225; CAC40; XETRA Dax and NASDAQ Composite

As mentioned above, the principal use of an index number is to measure the performance of a market. Some funds specifically attempt to track the value of the index whilst others aim to outperform. Thus, indices form an integral part of any benchmarking exercise.

In the summary below, the key indices for the various markets around the world are detailed.

When appraising performance, it is important to select the appropriate index against which to judge the fund manager. In some cases, this may involve creating a new index based on a mixture of investment types.

Name of Index	Country of Origin	Number of Shares	Notes
FTSE 100	UK	100	Based on top 100 UK shares by capitalisation, representing approx. 80% of the market
FTSE 250	UK	250	Based on next 250 shares
FTSE 350	UK	350	The combination of the 100 and 250 indices. Real-time indices are calculated for the industry baskets within the sector
FTSE All Share	UK	Around 900 full list companies	Represents approx. 98% of UK market capitalisation
Dow Jones Industrial Average	US	30	Provides a narrow view of the US stock market
S&P 500	US	500	Provides a wider view of the US stock market
Nikkei 225	Japan	225	
CAC 40	France	40	
Xetra Dax	Germany	30	
NASDAQ Composite	Domestic and International	3,000+	Includes over 3,000 international and domestic-based companies

7 SETS

Know how shares are traded on the London Stock Exchange – SETS

7.1 Introduction

The LSE decided, given that the diversity of shares on offer is so wide, that operating a single market structure for trading shares was not appropriate. Consequently different types of shares, with varying levels of liquidity, will trade via a variety of market systems, one of which is SETS.

SETS stands for **Stock Exchange Electronic Trading Service**. SETS is a fully automated order matching system. SETS covers the FTSE All Share Index stocks, Exchange Traded Funds (ETF), Exchange Traded Commodities (ETC) and the most liquid and frequently traded AIM stocks.

Those stocks tradable on SETS are referred to as **order book securities**. Only LSE member firms may place orders on SETS. Normal market hours for SETS are **08:00 to 16:30**, although the trading day is from 07:15 to 17:15.

7.2 The order book

The SETS screen only displays **limit orders** (orders to buy shares with a maximum price stated and orders to sell shares with a minimum price stated). Brokers can enter an order to be matched automatically with the limit orders displayed in order to buy or sell shares.

Below is an example order book for a SETS security.

Buy			Sell		
Time	Volume	Price	Price	Volume	Time
09:03	12,000	**174**	**175**	1,100	09:15
10:08	5,000	**174**	**176**	1,400	09:12
09:31	11,000	**173**	**176**	12,530	09:45
09:32	4,500	**173**	**176**	2,721	09:52
09:20	8,350	**172**	**177**	12,000	10:00
09:24	12,050	**172**	**177**	4,290	10:02
09:40	4,933	**172**			

Orders will appear on the screen in **price order**. For example, on the buy order side of the screen the highest prices appear first starting with 174 and then moving down.

If there are several orders at the same price then orders are prioritised by **time of input**. For example, there are three sell orders at 176 prioritised by time of input. The **size of order** is **not** a factor in prioritising orders, it is **first price, then time**. Volume of the order is irrelevant.

If a broker places an order to sell shares at 174, then the order will be automatically matched with the buy orders at 174. Matching will always start with the limit orders at the top of the list. Once matched, the buy orders are removed from the screen.

It should be noted that counterparties' names are not displayed on the system, nor when a trade is automatically executed are the relevant parties informed as to the identity of their counterparty. **LCH.Clearnet** (formerly the **London Clearing House**) acts as the **central counterparty** (offering a central counterparty service (CCS)) to all SETS trades. All automatically executed trades **novate** to LCH such that the buyer buys from the LCH and the seller sells to the LCH. The advantage of a CCS is that it provides pre and post-trade anonymity. When the LCH accounts in this manner, they are providing a central counterparty service (**CCS**).

7.3 Types of order

Only member firms of the LSE will be able to input orders into the system. There are a variety of different types of order that can be input.

- **Limit orders** – these are orders in which a worst acceptable price is specified. These are the **only** orders that will **appear on the screen** (with the exception of market orders during auction calls, see below).

  For example, if a member firm entered a buy order for 20,000 shares with a limit price of 176, this would match with the limit orders to sell shown in the screen above, as follows.

1,100	shares at 175
1,400	shares at 176
12,530	shares at 176
2,721	shares at 176
17,751	

  The unexecuted proportion of the deal (20,000 – 17,751 = 2,249 shares at 176) will then appear as the top buy order on the buy side of the order book.

  Limit orders may specify an expiry time and date (up to a maximum of **90 calendar days**). If no expiry date or time is specified, then the system will assume midnight on the current trading day as the expiry.

- **At best orders** – these are orders to buy or sell at whatever the best market price is. For example, an at best order to buy 10,000 shares will buy the 10,000 cheapest shares on offer in the system. In our example, this will give an execution pattern of 1,100 shares at 175 and 8,900 at 176. Partial execution is possible but any excess will be eliminated. Remember that only limit orders remain on the system during normal market hours.

- **Execute and eliminate** – similar to an 'at best' order, but with this type a limit price is also specified and a partial execution is possible. As much of the order as possible will be executed immediately and the remainder will be rejected. For example, if the order were to require the purchase of 4,000 at best but subject to a maximum price of 175, then the system would partially execute the bargain against the sell order for 1,100 shares at 175 and eliminate the rest, since it cannot at this stage be executed.

- **Fill or kill** – these are a variant of 'at best' or 'execute and eliminate' orders (where a limit price would be specified). If the order is entered as a fill or kill, no partial execution is possible. The order is either executed in full or entirely eliminated.

- **Market orders** – these are 'at best' orders that are entered into the system during an auction call period. **Auction call periods** take place during approximately the first ten and last five minutes of each day. They specify a volume to buy or sell but no price limit. They will have the highest priority for matching at the end of the auction call period in time entry order.

7.4 Summary of the SETS order types

Order type	Limit price required?	Partial execution allowed?	Unexecuted portion added to the order book?
Limit	Yes	Yes	Yes
At Best	No	Yes	No
Execute and Eliminate	Yes	Yes	No
Fill or Kill	Optional	No	No
Market Order	No	Yes	Yes

8 SETSqx AND SEAQ

Learning objective | **Know** how shares are traded on the London Stock Exchange – SEAQ/SETSqx

8.1 SETSqx

SETSqx (SETS 'quotes and crosses') is a trading platform for securities less liquid than those traded on SETS. SETSqx replaced SEAQ for all main market securities in 2007.

SETSqx combines a periodic electronic auction book with standalone quote driven market making. Uncrossings are scheduled at 08.00, 11.00, 15.00 and 16.35. Electronic orders can be named or anonymous and for the indicated securities order book executions will be centrally cleared. SETSqx allows members of the public to display limit orders: market makers and non-market makers can participate in auctions.

Market maker obligations: Mandatory Quotation Period from 08.00 until the end of closing auction obligation to quote up to 1 × Normal Market Size (NMS) – an order size that is set for each security.

8.2 Overview of SEAQ

SEAQ is the London Stock Exchange's service for the fixed interest (bond) market and AIM securities that are not traded on either SETS or SETSqx. **SEAQ** stands for the **Stock Exchange Automated Quotation System**.

While SETS is a system that overseas users can readily understand, SEAQ involves a very UK-specific approach that is not widely understood or trusted by overseas users. SEAQ is **not compliant** with the European **Markets in Financial Instruments Directive (MiFID)** because it contains no public limit order book. It was because of this that the LSE developed SETSqx, and SEAQ was replaced for main market securities.

Unlike SETS, there is no maximum spread regime in SEAQ. SEAQ effectively gives a monopoly over all incoming orders to the market makers since members of the public cannot submit limit orders which can match with each other. All deals on SEAQ are thus executed at the market makers' prices. This typically makes bid/ask spreads and therefore the 'transaction costs' of trading on SEAQ can be high.

On SETS, market participants can post electronic orders anonymously and directly participate in price formation while, on SEAQ, there is no ability for those who are not market makers to directly participate in the price formation process. The closing price is set by the mid- of the best market makers' bid and offer at 16:35.

In SEAQ, unlike SETS, there is no provision for a central counterparty.

All member firms of the LSE are broker-dealers. Broker-dealers have **dual capacity**. This means they can either act as agents on behalf of the customer or as principals dealing directly with the customer.

Some broker-dealers can elect to take on board a higher level of responsibility and become **market makers**. Market makers in the equity trading system are the focus of market activity, and their obligation is to ensure that there is always a **two-way price** (a price at which the market maker will buy and a price at which the market maker will sell) in the securities in which they are market makers.

The purpose of the screen-based system is to disseminate (display) prices at which market makers are willing to trade. Broker-dealers are then able to telephone through their orders based on the quoted prices.

Since a SEAQ security must have at least two market makers, it is referred to as a **competing market maker system**.

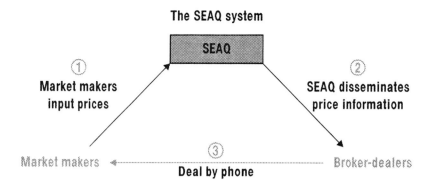

The SEAQ system

8.3 The SEAQ screen

First and foremost, the SEAQ system is a **price dissemination** system allowing the market makers to display the prices at which they will buy (the **bid price**) and sell (the **offer price**) shares.

The **yellow touch strip** shows the best prices available at the time.

8.4 The market maker quotes

Market makers are obliged to quote firm two-way prices throughout the **Mandatory Quote Period (MQP)**. The difference between the two prices is the spread and represents the market makers' profit. For example

MLSB   407-411

Market Maker   Bid   Offer
                    \   /
                  The Spread

The market makers can update their quote throughout the day.

9   EUROCLEAR UK & IRELAND: CREST

Understand the role played by Euroclear UK & Ireland in the clearing and settlement of equity trades: uncertificated transfers; participants (members, payment banks, registrars).

9.1 Introduction

Euroclear UK & Ireland (EUI) operates the UK's **dematerialised settlement system** which is generally known as **CREST**.

EUI is a **Recognised Clearing House (RCH)** and is regulated by the Financial Services Authority (FSA).

9.2 Settlement timings

EUI settles UK, various other European and NASDAQ equities and corporate loan stock denominated in sterling, US dollars and euros. The usual settlement period is **three business days** after the day of the bargain (referred to as T + 3). EUI also settles gilts, where the settlement period is T + 1. EUI now also has the ability to settle **money market instruments**.

Euroclear UK & Ireland settlement

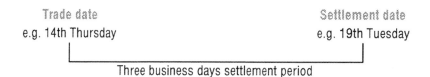

Trade date
e.g. 14th Thursday

Settlement date
e.g. 19th Tuesday

Three business days settlement period

9.3 CREST eligible securities

The **CREST** settlement system allows settlement of securities in certificated or uncertificated (dematerialised) form. However, the greatest benefit is derived from the EUI CREST system when settling uncertificated transfers, as the need for paper certificates is eliminated.

When a company participates in CREST, its securities are CREST-eligible. An investor has four choices of how to hold his shares.

- **Retaining paper certificates outside CREST**. This choice is much less efficient.

- **Holding the shares in dematerialised form within CREST**. The investor must become a CREST member or sponsored member. The investor has full legal ownership of the shares since his name will appear on the register of members.

- **Holding shares through a nominee company**. In this case, legal ownership passes to the nominee although the investor retains beneficial ownership. The nominee company can hold the shares in certificated form, or dematerialised form within CREST.

- Investors may continue to **hold shares in their own name** by using the LSE's EUI account, known as the LSE's Electronic Shareholding Service.

9.4 Overview of CREST participants

A CREST participant is anyone who has a formal relationship with EUI.

Euroclear UK & Ireland settlement

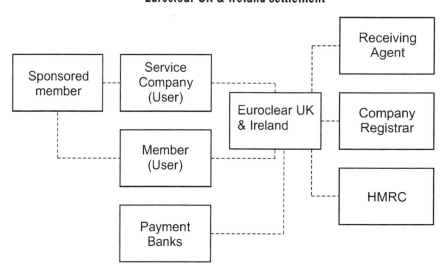

9.4.1 Users

Users are those who have the technical capacity to interface with CREST directly via their own computer systems.

9.4.2 User members

Members hold stock in dematerialised form in their own names within CREST. The member will be the legal owner of the shares (and have all associated legal rights) and it is the member's name which appears on the register kept by the company.

To qualify as a user member, the entity concerned must:

- Have access directly to EUI, i.e. be a 'user'

- Have a contract with a payment bank. The payment bank is under contract to make and receive payments in respect of the member's EUI activities

- Accept the terms and obligations of the EUI service

Examples of members would include LSE member firms (market makers, broker-dealers, stock borrowing and lending intermediaries, inter-dealer brokers), institutional investors and custodian banks.

9.4.3 Sponsored members

Sponsored members have all the same rights and responsibilities as user members. The only distinction is that sponsored members are not users since they do not have the technical capability to access EUI themselves.

Any instructions must be passed to a user member or service company (the 'sponsor') for onward communication with EUI.

Private investors may become sponsored members of EUI through their broker on payment of a fee. However, not all brokers offer this facility. As a result, some private investors will hold shares in EUI via a nominee, which will typically be their stockbroker, or the LSE's Electronic Shareholder Service.

9.4.4 Service companies

Service companies provide access to EUI for participants who do not have the specialist technology required to access EUI directly, e.g. sponsored members.

9.4.5 Payment banks

These participants have an obligation to guarantee payment for securities delivered to their customers through EUI. No money passes through CREST, as all payments take place outside the system. CREST merely records payment obligations via the accounting it provides.

9.4.6 Registrar

The role of the **company registrar** is to keep the legal record of the company's shareholders. Many companies use a third party to act as registrar. If the company decides to dematerialise its securities, the registrar must sign a service level agreement with EUI. This means that the registrar meets certain technical expertise requirements and time limits, for example:

- Responds to electronic instructions from EUI to update the register within **two hours** (either registration or rejection of the request). The electronic instruction sent by EUI is termed a **Register Update Request (RUR)**.

- Registration or rejection of stock deposit sets (the deposit of paper share certificates)

- Daily reconciliation with EUI of changes on the register, and periodic full reconciliations

9.5 Input and matching of instructions

Once trade details have been agreed, both counterparties will input settlement instructions. Whilst **no official time limit** exists for input, this is likely to be the trade date.

EUI will attempt to match settlement details once they have been received. No match will take place if the counterparty has not yet entered settlement instructions or the counterparty's instructions differ in any respect.

EUI will not send unsolicited information concerning the status of settlement instructions to members. It is therefore the members' responsibility to request updates and to ensure all settlement instructions are matched if proper settlement is to occur.

If unmatched transactions are not remedied by the member, they will be automatically deleted by EUI **60 business days** after input.

9.6 Settlement

On the intended settlement date, EUI will seek to settle matched transactions. Subject to the buying member having sufficient funds on their Cash Memorandum Account (CMA) and the selling member having sufficient stock in their stock accounts, EUI will proceed to settle the transaction by:

- Electronic transfer of stock
- Sending a RUR to the registrar

Creation of a payment (receipt) obligation on the buying (selling) member, which will result in a transfer of funds by the buyer's payment bank.

10 UK GOVERNMENT BONDS

Learning objective | **Know** the definition and features of UK government bonds; DMO maturity classifications; how they are issued.

10.1 Definition of a gilt

Governments often spend more money in a year than they raise in tax revenues. Consequently, they are obliged to borrow money to cover the deficit. Due to their high credit rating, they are able to borrow substantial sums with a wide range of maturities. The combination of this high credit rating and the size of the issues attracts investors. Government debt markets are the largest markets in the world in terms of activity.

A **government bond** is simply an acknowledgement of debt issued by the government with the promise to repay the debt at some date in the future. Over the life of the bond, the holder receives interest, referred to as the coupon. On maturity, the loan (the principal) is repaid. This is also referred to as the bond's nominal value, or par.

In the UK, the market in government debt is referred to as the **gilt-edged market** and the primary dealers in that market are referred to as gilt-edged market makers (GEMMs).

10.2 Gilt characteristics

UK GILTS - cash market

www.ft.com/gilts

Apr 27	Price £	Day's chng	W'ks chng	Int yield	Red yield	Red yield Day's chng	Red yield W'ks chng	Red yield Mth's chng	Red yield Year chng	52 Week High	52 Week Low	Amnt £m	Last xd date	Interest due
Shorts (Lives up to Five Years)														
Tr 4.75pc '10	100.47	-0.01	-0.06	4.73	0.50	+0.02	+0.02	+0.02	-0.20	104.58	100.36	21,285	28/11	7 Jun/Dec
Tr 8.25pc '10	103.28	+0.01	-0.07	6.05	0.52	-0.04	+0.02	-0.02	-0.36	108.54	103.21	6,719	16/11	25 May/Nov
Tr 3.25pc '11	103.56	+0.07	-0.05	3.14	1.01	-0.05	+0.08	+0.03	-0.74	115.22	102.55	15,747	28/11	7 Jun/Dec
Tr 4.25pc '11	103.09	+0.04	-0.01	4.12	0.64	-0.06	+0.00	-0.01	-0.54	105.94	102.90	23,651	24/02	7 Mar/Sep
Cn 9pc Ln '11	109.86	+0.04	-0.06	8.20	0.77	-0.05		-0.06	0.65	116.74	99.40	7,312	03/01	12 Jan/Jul
Tr 7.75pc '12 15 ✤	111.05	+0.09	-0.08	6.98	1.33	-0.08	+0.06	+0.02	0.78	115.53	110.92	407	17/01	26 Jan/Jul
Tr 5pc '12	106.92	+0.10	-0.06	4.68	1.22	-0.06	+0.08	+0.04	-0.80	108.57	106.56	26,867	24/02	7 Mar/Sep
Tr 5.25pc '12	107.93	+0.11	-0.07	4.87	1.42	-0.06	+0.08	+0.05	-0.77	109.51	107.21	25,612	28/11	7 Jun/Dec
Tr 9pc '12 ✤	116.58	+0.12	-0.11	7.73	1.55	-0.06	+0.08	+0.02	-0.72	122.09	114.92	204	27/01	6 Feb/Aug
Tr 8pc '13	119.64	+0.23	-0.08	6.70	2.02	-0.07	+0.07	0.01	-0.51	123.29	119.17	8,377	17/03	27 Mar/Sep
Tr 4.5pc '13	107.33	+0.18	-0.05	4.20	1.85	-0.07	+0.08	+0.03	-0.56	108.25	105.08	29,287	24/02	7 Mar/Sep
Tr 2.25pc '14	93.69	+0.21	-0.01	2.26	2.33	-0.06	+0.06	-0.02	+1.20	120.73	95.03	29,123	24/02	7 Mar/Sep
Tr 5pc '14	110.22	+0.23	-0.06	4.55	2.51	0.05	+0.05	0.00	+0.07	113.62	108.74	28,057	24/02	7 Mar/Sep
Tr 2.75pc '15	99.99	+0.24	-0.02	2.76	2.75	-0.05	+0.08	-0.08		100.35	98.00	19,381	13/01	22 Jan/Jul
Five to Ten Years														
Tr 4.75pc '15	109.13	+0.28		4.36	2.90	-0.05	+0.01		+0.10	112.34	107.64	29,548	24/00	7 Mar/Sep
Tr 8pc '15	125.27	+0.30	-0.04	6.37	2.96	-0.05	+0.01	0.01	+0.18	132.49	124.96	9,997	28/11	7 Jun/Dec
Tr 4pc '16	104.43	+0.30	+0.07	3.84	3.22	-0.05	-0.08	-0.07	+0.25	107.98	102.39	25,827	24/02	7 Mar/Sep
Tr 8.75pc '17	134.06	+0.30	+0.06	6.54	3.45	-0.04	-0.05	-0.08	+0.28	141.22	132.00	10,501	16/02	25 Feb/Aug
Ex 12pc '13-17 ✤	134.09	+0.25	-0.13	8.97	2.17	-0.07	+0.06	-0.01	-0.44	141.65	131.90	16	01/12	12 Jun/Dec
Tr 5pc '18	109.27	+0.27	+0.07	4.58	3.63	-0.04	-0.05	0.07	+0.39	114.07	105.08	25,388	24/02	7 Mar/Sep
Tr 3.75pc '19	98.40	+0.32	+0.18	3.82	3.95	0.04	0.06	-0.08		102.62	95.69	27,087	24/02	7 Mar/Sep
Tr 4.5pc '19	104.68	+0.31	+0.15	4.31	3.87	-0.04	-0.06	-0.06	+0.39	109.91	102.23	26,303	24/02	7 Mar/Sep
Tr 4.75pc '20	105.90	+0.35	+0.23	4.50	4.02	-0.04	-0.07	-0.05	+0.39	111.18	103.57	27,818	24/02	7 Mar/Sep
Ten to Fifteen Years														
Tr 8pc '21	134.45	+0.44	+0.19	5.97	4.11	0.04	0.07	-0.04	+0.49	143.34	93.74	22,686	24/02	7 Mar/Sep
Tr 4pc '22	97.79	+0.37	+0.27	4.11	4.24	-0.04	-0.07	0.08	+0.28	104.02	95.10	21,184	24/02	7 Mar/Sep
Tr 5pc '25	106.30	+0.47	+0.40	4.72	4.42	-0.04	-0.07	-0.06	+0.25	114.21	103.18	22,099	28/11	7 Jun/Dec
Over Fifteen Years														
Tr 4.25pc '27	97.11	+0.41	+0.31	4.40	4.49	0.03	-0.05	0.03	+0.25	105.74	94.48	21,425	24/02	7 Mar/Sep
Tr 8pc '28	119.33	+0.46	+0.35	5.05	4.46	-0.03	-0.05	0.04	+0.24	130.05	116.44	17,932	28/11	7 Jun/Dec
Tr 4.75pc '30	103.01	+0.41	+0.29	4.63	4.52	-0.03	-0.05	-0.06	+0.22	120.13	99.71	21,285	28/11	7 Jun/Dec
Tr 4.25pc '32	96.38	+0.41	+0.30	4.43	4.51	-0.03	-0.05	-0.06	+0.25	105.60	93.22	24,618	26/11	7 Jun/Dec
Tr 4.5pc '34	99.13	+0.44	+0.32	4.56	4.56	-0.03	0.05	-0.06		109.39	95.96	11,159	24/02	7 Mar/Sep
Tr 4.25pc '36	95.43	+0.36	+0.20	4.47	4.55	0.03	-0.04	0.07	+0.19	104.70	92.54	20,227	28/11	7 Jun/Dec
Tr 4.75pc '38	103.35	+0.36	+0.15	4.61	4.54	-0.02	-0.03	-0.06	+0.23	113.74	94.82	22,759	24/02	7 Mar/Sep
Tr 4.25 '39	95.01	+0.31	+0.11	4.48	4.56	-0.02	-0.02	-0.06	+0.20	105.13	90.21	16,418	24/00	7 Mar/Sep
Tr 4.5pc '42	96.58	+0.32	+0.11	4.53	4.52	-0.02	0.02	-0.06	+0.20	109.59	96.70	19,120	28/11	7 Jun/Dec
Tr 4.25pc '46	95.62	+0.34	+0.10	4.46	4.50	-0.02	0.02	-0.05	+0.17	108.04	92.28	17,751	28/11	7 Jun/Dec
Tr 4.25pc '49	95.50	+0.23	+0.07	4.47	4.49	-0.02	-0.01	-0.05	+0.17	105.56	92.37	16,436	28/11	7 Jun/Dec
Tr 4.25pc '55	95.61	+0.36	+0.10	4.46	4.48	-0.02	-0.01	-0.05	+0.19	106.02	92.00	20,147	28/11	7 Jun/Dec
Tr 4pc 60	90.34	+0.35	+0.10	4.44	4.49	0.02	0.01	-0.05		100.61	88.27	11,500	13/01	22 Jan/Jul
Undated														
Cons 4pc ✤	76.42	+0.07	-0.08	5.24	5.23‡	-0.01	-0.01	-0.03	+0.38	83.90	74.81	266		
War Ln 3.5pc	71.95	-0.08	-0.24	4.86	4.86‡	+0.01	+0.00	-0.00	+0.39	109.91	70.46	1,938	22/11	1 Jun/Dec
Cn 3.5 pc '51 Aft	70.50	+0.06	-0.09	4.97	4.96‡	-0.01	-0.01	-0.03	+0.38	81.79	68.93	17		
Tr 3pc '66 Aft	59.36	+0.06	-0.07	5.06	5.05‡	-0.01	-0.01	-0.03	+0.38	70.03	58.06	40		
Cons 2.5pc ✤	50.67	+0.05	-0.06	4.94	4.93‡	-0.01	-0.01	-0.03	+0.38	59.96	49.53	181		
Tr 2.5pc	51.39	-0.06	-0.18	4.86	4.87‡	+0.01	+0.00	-0.02	+0.39	79.23	50.33	423		
Index-linked				(1)	(2)									
2.5pc '11 (74.6)	309.29	+0.13	0.25						-0.63	311.55	289.51	4,802	14/02	23 Feb/Aug
2.5pc '13 (89.2)	271.49	+0.24	-0.06						-1.01	273.23	242.30	7,620	07/02	16 Feb/Aug
2.5pc '16 (81.6)	303.95	+0.50	-1.13	-0.01	0.18	-0.03	+0.03	-0.12	-0.90	305.77	272.55	7,982	17/01	26 Jan/Jul
1.25pc '17 † (193.725)	106.82	+0.17	-0.45	0.34	0.34	-0.02		0.19	-0.61	297.45	98.77	11,434	11/11	22 May/Nov
2.5pc 20 (83.0)	306.36	+0.04	-0.63	0.60	0.72	0.04	0.02	-0.11	-0.47	310.76	109.37	6,584	07/04	16 Apr/Oct
1.875pc '22† (205.65806)	113.15	+0.52	-0.43	0.77	0.77	-0.04	+0.01	-0.12	-0.40	259.86	103.71	10,004	11/11	22 May/Nov
2.5pc '24 (97.7)	268.62	+1.32	-0.96	0.84	0.93	-0.04	+0.03	-0.02	-0.34	271.18	102.47	6,827	06/01	17 Jan/Jul
1.25pc '27† (194.06667)	105.52	+0.64	0.63	0.91	0.91	-0.04	+0.05	+0.04	-0.28	111.93	97.53	11,228	11/11	22 May/Nov
4{1/8}pc '30 (135.1)	255.05	+1.30	1.49			-0.03	+0.05	+0.05	0.25	261.33	150.02	5,207	13/01	22 Jan/Jul
1.25pc '32† (217.13226)	107.42	+1.04	-0.76			-0.05	+0.07	+0.08	-0.24	141.10	101.27	9,728	28/11	7 Jun/Dec
2pc '35 (173.6)	155.18	+0.78	-1.78			-0.03	+0.09	+0.08	-0.09	166.84	91.98	9,738	17/01	26 Jan/Jul
1.125pc '37† (202.24286)	107.00	+0.61	-1.63			-0.02	+0.10	+0.08	-0.10	150.88	91.03	10,927	11/11	22 May/Nov
0.625pc '40 (216.52258)	94.17		-1.50			-0.03	+0.09	+0.08		105.01	89.98	3,500		22 Mar/Sep
0.625pc '42† (212.46452)	95.11	+0.72	-1.53			-0.03	+0.10	+0.10		145.76	92.41	6,718	11/11	22 May/Nov
0.75pc '47† (207.76667)	100.88	+0.74	-1.69			-0.02	+0.10	+0.11	-0.02	161.30	36.37	6,573	11/11	22 May/Nov
0.5pc 50† (213.40000)	92.53	+0.84	-1.65			-0.03	+0.09	+0.10		106.91	89.73	5,000	11/03	22 Mar/Sep
1.25pc '55† (192.20000)	121.92	+1.14	-2.15			0.03	+0.09	+0.10	+0.02	143.29	110.60	5,723	11/11	22 May/Nov

All UK Gilts are Tax free to non-residents on application. xd Ex dividend. Closing mid-prices are shown in pounds per £100 nominal of stock. Weekly percentage changes are calculated on a Friday to Friday basis. Gilt benchmarks and most liquid stocks, are shown in bold type. A full list of Gilts can be found daily on ft.com/bond&rates.
Prospective real redemption rate on projected inflation of (1) 5% and (2) 3% (b) Figures in parentheses show RPI base for indexing (ie 8 months prior to issue and, for gilts issued since September 2005, 3 months prior to issue) and have been adjusted to reflect rebasing of RPI to 100 in January 1987. Conversion factor 3.945. RPI for Sep 2009: 215.3 and for Apr 2009 211.5. D For those bonds indicated, with a 3m lag, the 'clean' price shown has no inflation adjustment. The yield is calculated using no inflation assumption. ‡ Running yield.

Source: REUTERS Ltd.

As you will see from the extract above (from the *Financial Times* website on 10 March 2009), a wide variety of gilts is available.

Let us take a typical issue and examine the key features.

Name	Coupon	Maturity	Price
Exchequer	12%	2013-17	@ £143.22

10.2.1 Coupon

The coupon is the **rate of interest** that will be paid **on the nominal value amount** of the stock outstanding. In the UK, the convention is for this coupon to be paid on a **semi-annual basis** in equal instalments. However, there is an exception to this rule: **2½% Consolidated Stock**, which pays coupon on a **quarterly basis**.

Gilts pay coupons **gross**, i.e. without any withholding tax being deducted. Investors are liable for income tax at the savings rate of tax, which will depend on their particular tax circumstances. However, an individual may **elect** for their own convenience to receive the coupon net of **20% withholding tax**. The cheque paying the coupon may be referred to as a **warrant** – not to be confused with warrants on shares, which we cover when we look at derivatives in a later Chapter.

Example: Gilt Coupon

Calculate the next coupon on £440 nominal value (NV) of Treasury 8% 2021, where the investor has made an election to receive the coupon net of withholding tax.

Coupon   = Nominal value $\times$ Coupon $\times$ ½ $\times$ (1 – Tax rate)

$\qquad$ = [£440 $\times$ (8% $\times$ ½) $\times$ (1 – 20%)]

$\qquad$ = £440 $\times$ 0.08 $\times$ ½ $\times$ 0.80

$\qquad$ = £14.08

This calculation accounts for the semi-annual coupon payment convention and also adjusts for a 20% withholding tax deducted at source.

10.2.2 Settlement of gilts

Gilts settle T + 1, i.e. one business day after the trade.

10.3 Gilts – issue methods

The **Debt Management Office (DMO)** is part of HM Treasury and is responsible for ensuring that the government is able to borrow the money it requires to fund the Public Sector Net Cash Requirement (PSNCR). The gilt market can be seen as the most important source of financing open to the Government.

The DMO controls the issue of gilts into the market place and uses a variety of methods depending upon the circumstances it faces at any time. **Tenders** were very popular until the late 1980s: applicants would state how much of the nominal value they wanted and how much they were prepared to pay. The DMO would then make an allocation of the new issue among the participants, with all of them paying a common strike price.

After 1987, the DMO began to use mainly an **auction** system, where all the applicants end up paying the price they bid. As with the tender, highest bids are awarded first.

There is also the facility to submit **non-competitive bids**. A non-competitive bid does not contain a price and is allocated at the average of the competitive bid prices that have been accepted by the DMO. The maximum amount of stock that can be applied for under a non-competitive bid, by a non-market maker, is £500,000 nominal.

Gilts are referred to as **registered** securities. The register is maintained by Computershare Investor Services plc, known as Computershare, on behalf of the DMO.

10.4 Maturity

Gilt-edged stocks are classified with respect to their maturity dates. This is the date on which the government has agreed to repay the debt.

The official DMO definitions are:

- **Shorts:** Gilts with seven years or less to run
- **Mediums:** Gilts with between seven and 15 years until redemption
- **Longs:** Gilts with over 15 years to go to redemption

10.5 Advantages and disadvantages of investing in Government bonds

Advantages	Disadvantages
- The credit rating of the UK government - The 'guaranteed' return of capital - They provide an income stream - Coupon is paid gross (but taxable) - Potential tax-free capital gains	- Relatively low return due to them being low risk - Coupon is subject to income tax - Value will fall if interest rates rise

11 OTHER FIXED INTEREST SECURITIES

ning objectives   **Know** the definitions and features of the following types of bond: domestic; foreign; Eurobond; asset-backed securities; zero coupon; convertible
Know the advantages and disadvantages of investing in different types of bond
Be able to calculate the flat yield of a bond
Understand the role of credit rating agencies and the differences between investment and non-investment grades

11.1 Corporate bonds

The market in fixed interest debt issued by companies in the UK is relatively small compared to international markets. The limited interest reflects in part the risk attached but also the UK investment market's strong focus on equities (companies' ordinary shares).

Due to the low level of liquidity in this market, there are relatively few issues which secure the required volume or market makers to trade through SEAQ. Thus, much trading is carried out on a matched bargain basis.

Corporate bonds settle **three business days** after the day of trade **(T + 3)**.

Many corporate bonds are issued with a fixed coupon. However, there are long-term instruments of corporate debt issued with a variable rate of interest, i.e. the coupon is reset periodically and will change as underlying lending rates change. Such instruments are known as **FRNs, Floating Rate Notes. LIBOR, London Interbank Offered Rate**, is normally the benchmark for FRNs.

Some corporate bonds are issued with **warrants** to make them more attractive to investors. A warrant is an instrument that gives an investor the **right to buy new shares** in the company.

If a UK company issues bonds into the UK market in sterling, they are referred to as **domestic bonds**. If the issuer is foreign, they would be known as **foreign bonds**. Such a bond is specifically known as a 'bulldog bond', where the foreign issuer is raising sterling within the UK. If, for example, it was a foreign issuer raising dollars in the US, it would be called a 'Yankee bond'.

Since the introduction of Eurobonds, new issues of foreign bonds have declined.

11.2 Eurobonds

In essence, a **Eurobond** is simply a debt instrument issued by a borrower (typically a government or a large company) normally outside of the country in which currency it is denominated. For example, a US dollar Eurobond could be issued anywhere in the world except for the US. As such, a better name for it might be an 'international bond'. As mentioned above, Eurobonds frequently carry no security other than the high name and credit rating of the issuer. Another important feature of bonds issued in this market is that for the most part they are issued in **bearer form**, with no formal register of ownership held by the company.

It should be noted that for a number of pragmatic reasons, the clearing houses in the Euromarkets do maintain a form of record of ownership but that this record is not normally open either to government or tax authorities.

The Eurobond market is, in effect, an international market in debt. Companies issuing debt in the Eurobond market have their securities traded all around the world and are not limited to one domestic market place. Many issues of Eurobonds also involve cross-currency swaps, allowing the issuer to swap the currency of the Eurobond. For example, an Irish company may, for liquidity purposes, issue a US dollar Eurobond and then swap those dollars into euros.

11.3 Credit ratings

When an investor buys a corporate bond, the investor is the lender and the bond is the issuer's debt.

The investor needs to consider:

- The borrower's credit history
- If the borrower will default
- If the investor is being compensated for the risk they are taking

To answer these questions, a stringent set of criteria is used to assess the creditworthiness of the bond.

All issues except those companies or corporations with high name recognition (household names) require a **rating** from one of the credit rating agencies. The credit rating gives an indication to potential investors of the level of security that they can find in a particular issue.

Credit rating agencies, and the ratings they have given to certain securities such as those asset-backed securities backed by **mortgages** (see below), have been blamed in part by some for **problems** arising in financial markets during **2007 and 2008**.

The three main agencies offering credit ratings are **Moody's, Standard & Poor's** and **Fitch**, whose rating systems, divided into **investment grade** and **non-investment grade**, are shown in the following Table.

Investment grade (Prime)			Non-investment grade (Non-prime or 'Junk')		
Standard & Poor's	Moody's	Fitch	Standard & Poor's	Moody's	Fitch
AAA	Aaa	AAA	BB+	Ba1	BB+
AA+	Aa1	AA+	BB	Ba2	BB
AA	Aa2	AA	BB–	Ba3	BB–
AA–	Aa3	AA–	B+	B1	B+
A+	A1	A+	B	B2	B
A	A2	A	B–	B3	B–
A–	A3	A–	CCC	Caa	CCC
BBB+	Baa1	BBB+	CC	Ca	
BBB	Baa2	BBB	C	C	
BBB–	Baa3	BBB–	D		

Taking Standard & Poor's ratings for example, BBB and above are **investment grades**. Debt rated BBB is regarded as having an adequate capacity to pay interest and repay principal. Adverse economic conditions or changing circumstances are more likely to lead to a weakened capacity to pay interest and repay principal for debt in this category than in higher rated categories.

Again with the example of Standard & Poor's ratings, **non-investment grade** debt rated BB, B, CCC, CC and C is regarded, on balance, as predominantly speculative with respect to capacity to pay interest and repay principal in accordance with the terms of the obligation. While such debt will likely have some quality and protective characteristics, these are outweighed by large uncertainties or major risk exposures to adverse conditions.

11.4 Zero coupon bonds

These bonds carry no coupon rate. As with Treasury bills, they are issued at a **discount to their face value**. The discount reflects the interest that is liable over the life of the bond. For example, a **zero coupon bond** with a repayment value of £100 in two years' time may be issued today at £90, the £10 gain at redemption representing the equivalent of £5 of interest each year.

11.5 Convertibles

A **convertible loan stock** is a fixed interest loan stock or a preference share which carries the right to **convert into ordinary shares** on the terms and conditions set out in the Articles of Association. The stockholder has the right, but not the obligation, to convert within stipulated time limits. If conversion rights are not exercised by the expiry date, the stock will revert to a conventional dated loan stock.

The holder of a convertible loan stock has a legal right to receive his fixed interest in the same way as any other creditor is entitled to money owing. In addition the loan stock is an external liability which must be met in full in any liquidation before the shareholders receive a penny. However, should the company prosper, the loan stockholder can obtain an equity stake by converting.

Usually a convertible loan stock will be priced above a comparable 'straight' loan stock because of the attraction of the conversion option.

11.6 Asset-backed securities (ABSs)

Asset-backed securities (ABSs) are constructed by packaging together a group of securities and then issuing a new security whose purchaser has a claim against the cash flows generated by the original package. The process is known as '**securitisation**'. ABSs are securities that are backed by one or more particular assets(s), such as credit card debt, mortgages and other loans. They are 'backed' by assets because the cash flows from these underlying assets are the primary source of payments on the asset-backed securities.

The overall market is known as the **Collateralised Debt Obligation (CDO)** market, where the ABS shifts credit risk on a pool of homogenous assets, such as mortgage loans, credit cards or car loans.

A **collateralised bond obligation (CBO)** is where the ABS is typically backed by a pool of non-investment grade bonds (high yield bonds), emerging market bonds or corporate bank loans.

Where the pool is exclusively made up of bank loans, it is referred to as a **collateralised loan obligation (CLO)**.

In the financial turmoil and property value declines of 2008 and 2009, the poor quality and uncertain valuation of many ABSs linked to mortgages caused problems for many financial institutions.

11.7 Flat yield

The **flat yield**, running yield, income yield or interest yield is a simple measure of the return given by a particular bond. All it does is to express the annual income that you receive (note here that it is the gross income, before the deduction of tax) over the amount that you would have to pay for the bond (i.e. its market price).

Exam tip

$$\frac{\text{Gross coupon}}{\text{Market price}} \times 100 = \text{Flat yield}$$

You could be expected to be able to perform this calculation in the exam.

Example: Yield calculation

What is the income yield of a 7% gilt redeemable in two years, if it is trading at £104?

Solution

$$\frac{£7 \text{ coupon}}{£104 \text{ price}} \times 100 = 6.73\% \text{ return}$$

For an investment of £104 the investor will receive an annual coupon of £7 (gross), which is an effective return on their money of 6.73%.

Whilst the income or flat yield is an important measure of the value of a bond, it is not perfect. One of the principal drawbacks is that it ignores the concept of redemption and is therefore suitable if you are interested in income only (e.g. a non-tax paying pensioner). A solution to this is to calculate the gross redemption yield. The income yield is however a valuable tool when calculating yields on bonds that pay coupons until the end of time. These bonds are known as irredeemable bonds or perpetuities.

11.8 Advantages and disadvantages of investing in bonds

Advantages	Disadvantages
■ They provide an income stream ■ Rank higher than shares should a company be forced into liquidation ■ Higher yield than Government bonds	■ Higher risk than Government bonds (hence higher yield) ■ Coupon subject to income tax ■ Value will fall if interest rates rise

12 MONEY MARKET INSTRUMENTS

Know the difference between a capital market instrument and a money market instrument
Know the definition and features of the following: Treasury Bill; Commercial Paper; Certificate of Deposit
Know the advantages and disadvantages of investing in money market instruments

12.1 Overview of the market

The money market is a complex market where banks balance their liquidity requirements and the Bank of England controls the interest rate.

Essentially, this is a short-term **wholesale** cash market. The instruments that trade on the **money market**, such as Treasury Bills, are thus short-term instruments, which directly contrasts, in maturity terms, with the **capital market** instruments of government and corporate bonds that we have just discussed.

The London money market

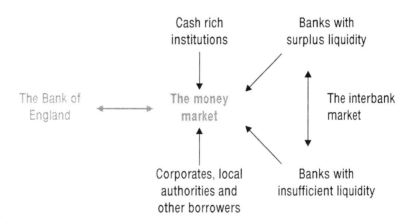

The key players in the money markets are the banks. Banks make their money by taking in deposits from savers and lending them out at a higher rate to borrowers. In doing so, the bank always has to ensure that they have enough liquid assets to meet the demands of their investors for cash. The bank will achieve this by carrying a proportion of the money invested in the form of cash and will also put other money on deposit, at very short notice. The remainder of their liquidity will be held in the form of short-term investments such as treasury bills, which are easily convertible into cash.

Banks can also manage their liquidity via the interbank markets. Those banks with surplus funds can earn a return by passing them to banks short of funds. The average rate at which funds can be raised is **LIBOR (London Interbank Offered Rate)** and the average rate earned on deposits is **LIBID (London Interbank Bid Rate).**

12.2 Treasury Bills and Commercial Paper

The most important form of UK bill is issued by the DMO, and is known as a **Treasury bill or a T-bill**. This is an obligation to repay a set amount of money, normally in **91 days' time** and, as with all bills, is issued at a discount to its face value. For example, the DMO might issue a three-month £1m Treasury bill. This would be issued to the market at a discount: the market might be prepared to pay £990,000 now in order to receive £1m in three months' time. The riskier the investment, the greater the amount of discount required by the purchaser. The minimum denomination of a Treasury bill is **£25,000**. Treasury bills are sold by tender every Friday. The DMO also sells the bills denominated in euros by monthly tender.

If this is issued by a company it is called **Commercial Paper (CP)**. The lifespan of commercial paper is from eight to 365 days. CP pays no interest, instead trading at a discount to nominal value. The discount reflects credit risk and time to maturity. Thus a CP is nothing other than a short-term debt instrument issued by a company, commonly guaranteed by an eligible bank.

12.3 Certificates of Deposit (CDs)

A **Certificate of Deposit (CD)** is a long-term bank account which is itself transferable. For example, a bank issues a £1m CD carrying an interest rate of 5%. This will redeem in one year's time when the holder of the CD will receive £1,050,000 (principal plus interest).

The certificate of ownership issued by the bank is a bearer document and can be transferred. The holder of the CD can, if they wish to raise their cash immediately, sell the CD into the market place and receive back an amount which is a discount to the final end value of £1,050,000. The size of the discount will reflect both the time to maturity and current rates of interest.

12.4 Advantages and disadvantages of investing in money market instruments

Advantages	Disadvantages
■ Very safe – issued by the Government or guaranteed by eligible banks/strong companies	■ Low return/yield
■ Very liquid market	■ High minimum investment levels makes them restrictive to private investors
■ Suitable for shorter term investors, e.g. general insurance companies	■ Gain in value is subject to income tax

CHAPTER ROUNDUP

- A company is an entity owned by its shareholders (members) who may vote at company meetings, and is run by its directors.

- A private company (Ltd) is prohibited from offering its shares to the general public, while a public company (plc) can do this.

- 'Equities' are ordinary shares, carrying equal rights to a share in profits. Preference shares do not usually carry voting rights but normally provide fixed dividends, and these have priority over ordinary share dividends.

- A shareholder will hope that the value of the shares increase (to create a capital gain) as well as possibly receiving income from dividends. If the company fails, the shares could become worthless.

- Holding shares involves price risk (the price may fall), liquidity risk (it may not be possible to trade at acceptable prices sometimes) and issuer risk (if a company defaults).

- A bonus issue effectively increases the number of shares but decreases the share price pro rata. A rights issue is an issue of new shares, to raise more money for the company.

- A public company may obtain a full listing on the LSE, or it may join the more lightly regulated Alternative Investment Market (AIM).

- Share price indices, such as the FTSE 100 Index ('the Footsie') and the Dow Jones Industrial Average ('the Dow'), track the aggregated value of a sample of shares.

- SETS is a fully automated system for matching buyers and sellers of shares, covering all but the least liquid UK shares.

- Euroclear UK & Ireland (EUI) operates CREST, a dematerialised settlement system, dispensing with the need to hold paper certificates.

- On behalf of the Government, the Debt Management Office controls the issue of gilts: UK government debt.

- Fixed interest securities also include securities issued by companies and other corporate bodies (corporate bonds).

- The money market is for the trading of short-term wholesale cash instruments such as Treasury Bills, and the key players are banks.

TEST YOUR KNOWLEDGE

Check your knowledge of the Chapter here, without referring back to the text.

1. The key difference between a limited company ('Ltd') and a public limited company ('plc') is in respect of:
    A   Limitation of shareholders' liability
    B   Ability of company to offer shares to the general public
    C   Stock Exchange listed status
    D   Ability of company to buy back its own shares

2. What name is given to the risk of being unable to trade in securities in normal quantities at a particular time?

3. Define 'issuer risk'.

4. Give two alternative terms for a 'bonus issue'.

5. What name is given to the price at which a share should trade after a rights issue, reflecting the dilution involved?

6. Which of the following is *not* normally an advantage for a company in obtaining listed status?
    A   Reduced likelihood of being taken over
    B   Increased prestige
    C   Enhanced ability to raise funds
    D   Ability to offer own shares as part-consideration in a takeover

7. Suppose that, compared with yesterday's values, the FTSE 100 index rises by X% and the FTSE 250 Index rises by Y%, which is an amount greater than X%. What can we say about the FTSE 350 Index?
    A   It must have risen by less than X%
    B   It must have risen by more than Y%
    C   It must have risen by an amount that is between X% and Y%
    D   None of the conclusions A, B or C can be drawn

8. What does the acronym 'SETS' stand for?

9. What term is used for an order for securities which must either be executed in the total amount ordered or alternatively cancelled?

10. Market makers are obliged to quote firm two-way prices for amounts up to the NMS throughout MQP. What do 'NMS' and 'MQP' stand for?

11. Which agency that is part of HM Treasury handles the issue of gilts?

12. What is the normal settlement period for corporate bonds?

13. What is the name given to the short-term wholesale cash market?

TEST YOUR KNOWLEDGE: ANSWERS

1. B is the correct answer. Note that a 'plc' may or may not be listed.

    See Section 1.2

2. Liquidity risk.

    See Section 2.2

3. Issuer risk can be defined as the risk of default when one institution holds debt securities issued by another company, which then defaults on its obligation to pay.

    See Section 2.2

4. You could have mentioned: scrip issues, capitalisation issues, cap issues, free issues.

    See Section 3.2

5. The theoretical ex-rights price.

    See Section 3.4.1

6. A is the correct answer: listed status will generally increase the possibility of a company being taken over.

    See Sections 4.1 and 4.2

7. C is the correct answer. The FTSE 350 Index combines the FTSE 100 and the FTSE 250. Therefore, the rise in the FTSE 350 must be between the rises on the two other indices.

    See Section 6.2

8. Stock Exchange Electronic Trading Service.

    See Section 7.1

9. 'Fill or kill'.

    See Section 7.3

10. 'Normal Market Size' and 'Mandatory Quote Period'.

    See Section 8.1

11. The Debt Management Office.

    See Section 10.3

12. T + 3.

    See Section 11.1

13. The money market.

    See Section 12.1

3

Derivatives

In this chapter, we explain enough about the workings of futures and options – types of derivative – to understand their role for the investor. Bear in mind that the availability of derivatives increases the flexibility available to the investor in executing an investment strategy, whether the investor is interested in reducing risks, or in taking on additional risk in the hope of a higher return.

This involves defining some of the special terminology of derivatives and looking at examples of how derivatives can lead to particular profit/loss outcomes.

We will also consider warrants and interest rate swaps, however, you should note that warrants are technically classified as securities since they trade on the London Stock Exchange.

CHAPTER CONTENTS

	Page
1 Uses and Applications of Derivatives	61
2 Futures	62
3 Traded Equity Options	63
4 Risks Summary: Futures and Options	67
5 Interest Rate Swaps	67
Chapter Roundup	69
Test Your Knowledge	71

CHAPTER LEARNING OBJECTIVES

Derivatives uses

■ **Understand** the uses and application of derivatives

Terminology

■ **Understand** the following terms:

- Long
- Short
- Open
- Close
- Holder
- Writing
- Premium
- Covered
- Naked
- OTC
- Exchange-traded

Futures

■ **Know** the definition and function of a future

Options

■ **Know** the definition and function of an option

■ **Understand** the following terms

- Calls
- Puts

Swaps

■ **Know** the definition and function of an interest rate swap

BPP
LEARNING MEDIA

1 USES AND APPLICATIONS OF DERIVATIVES

Learning objectives | **Understand** the uses and application of derivatives
Understand the following terms: OTC, exchange-traded

Derivatives is a term used to encompass products such as **futures**, **options** and **swaps**, which derive their value from various factors which include the movement in price of an underlying asset.

In the minds of the general public, and indeed those of many people involved in the financial services industry, financial instruments such as futures and options are thought of as very complicated. They are also thought of as having little to do with the real world. Television coverage showing pictures of young traders in brightly coloured jackets, shouting at each other in an apparent frenzy, makes it difficult to imagine that what they are engaged in may be of value to the smooth functioning of the economy.

At the heart of futures and options is the concept of **deferred delivery**. Both instruments allow you, albeit in slightly different ways, to agree **today** the price at which you will buy or sell an asset at some date in the future. This is unlike normal everyday transactions. When we go to a supermarket, we pay our money and take immediate delivery of our goods. Why would someone wish to agree at a price today for delivery at some time in the future? The answer is **certainty**.

Imagine a farmer growing a crop of wheat. To grow such a crop costs money – money for seed, labour, fertiliser and so on. All this expenditure takes place with no certainty that when the crop is eventually harvested the price at which the wheat is sold will cover these costs. This is obviously a risky thing to do and many farmers will be unwilling to take on this burden.

How can this uncertainty be avoided?

By using futures or options, the farmer will be able to agree **today** a price at which the crop will ultimately be sold, in maybe four or six months' time. This enables the farmer to achieve a minimum sale price for his crop. He is no longer subject to fluctuations in wheat prices. He knows what price his wheat will bring and can thus plan his business accordingly. We say that he has 'hedged his bets', hence we say that futures and options may be used to **hedge** the risk of a position.

From their origins in the agricultural world, futures and options have become available on a wide range of other assets, from metals and crude oil to bonds and equities. To understand futures and options properly requires some application. There is much terminology to master, and definitions to be understood, but at heart they are really quite simple. They are products which allow you to fix a price today that assets may be bought or sold at a future date.

A study of derivatives would not be complete without breaking through some of the jargon used on the derivatives markets. Bulls and bears are often mentioned when considering strategies for a **speculator**. A **bullish** investor believes the price of the asset or commodity will **rise over time.** Conversely, a **bearish** investor believes the price of an asset or commodity will **fall over time**. When used in a speculative manner derivatives have the potential to offer very high returns but may expose the investor to very high risks. Strategies are expanded upon later in this section.

An **exchange-traded derivative** is one that is packaged in a standardised way, in respect of the contract size and dates for example. An 'over the counter' or **OTC derivative** is one that has been specially negotiated with a financial institution, to fit the needs of a particular client.

2 FUTURES

Know the definition and function of a future
Understand the following terms: long, short, open, close

2.1 Definition of a future

A **future** is an agreement to buy or sell a standard quantity of a specified asset on a fixed future date at a price agreed today.

There are two parties to a futures contract: a buyer and a seller.

- The buyer of a future enters into an **obligation** to buy on a specified date.
- The seller of a future is under an **obligation** to sell on a future date.

These obligations relate to a **standard quantity** of a **specified** asset on a **fixed future date** at a **price agreed today**.

Futures are **tradable**, so although the contract obligates the buyer to buy and the seller to sell, these obligations can be **offset** by undertaking an equal and opposite trade in the market.

For example, suppose a farmer in April has sold one September wheat future at £120 per tonne. If subsequently, in August, the farmer decides he does not wish to sell his wheat, but would prefer to use the grain to feed his cattle, he simply buys one September future at the then prevailing price in August. His original sold position is now offset by a bought position, leaving him with no outstanding delivery obligations for September.

This offsetting is common in future markets; very few contracts run through to delivery.

2.2 Using futures

Various people use futures. Some, like the wheat farmer, may use them to reduce risk. Others do so seeking high returns – and for this, are willing to take high risks. Futures markets are, in fact, wholesale markets in risk, markets in which risks are transferred from the cautious to those with more adventurous (or reckless) spirits.

The users fall into one of two categories: the **hedger** or the **speculator.**

- The hedger is someone seeking to reduce risk
- The speculator is a risk taker seeking large profits

A transaction in which a future is purchased to **open** a position is known as a **long position**. Thus, the purchase of the oil future would be described as **going long of the future** or simply **long**.

Conversely, when a future is sold to open a position, this is described as **going short** or simply, **short**.

As previously discussed, most futures do not run until delivery date but are **closed out** to extinguish their obligations. **Opening purchases** are thus extinguished by **closing sales**, while **opening sales** are closed out by **closing purchases**.

3 TRADED EQUITY OPTIONS

ing objectives **Know** the definition and function of an option
Understand the following terms: calls, puts, long, short, holder, writing, premium, covered, naked

3.1 Definition

An **option** is a contract that confers the right, but not the obligation, to buy or sell an asset at a given price, on or before a given date.

3.2 Terminology and principles

In the definition above, an option is described as being the right, but not the obligation, to **buy** or **sell**. The right to buy and the right to sell are given different names.

- The right to buy an asset is known as a **call option**.
- The right to sell an asset is known as a **put option**.

The right to buy (call) or sell (put) is held by the person buying the option, who is also known as the **holder**. The person selling an option is known as a **writer**.

The price at which an options contract gives the right to buy (call) or sell (put) is known as the **exercise price** or **strike price**.

It is important to understand the relationship between **holders** and **writers** of options. The following diagram illustrates this for a call option. The holder has paid a 10p **premium** for the right but not the obligation to buy a share for the agreed price of £1 on or before a date in three months' time.

Call Option

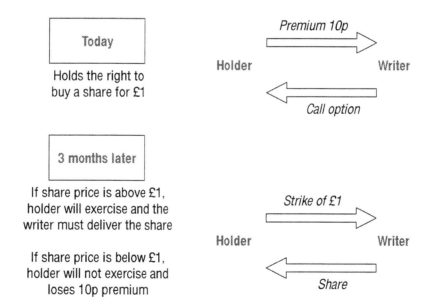

The first thing to understand is the flow of the **premium**. The premium is the cost of an option paid by the holder and received by the writer.

When option holders wish to take up their rights under the contract they are said to **exercise** the contract. In return for receiving the premium, the writer agrees to fulfil the terms of the contract, which of course are different for calls and puts.

Call writers agree to deliver the asset underlying the contract if 'called' upon to do so. For a call option, this means that the writer must deliver the underlying asset for which he will receive the fixed amount of cash stipulated in the original contract.

Call option writers run very considerable risks. In return for receiving the option premium, they are committed to delivering the underlying asset at a fixed price. As the price of the asset could, in theory, rise infinitely, they could be forced to buy the underlying asset in the market at a high price and to deliver it to the call option's holder at a much lower value. Therefore, we can describe their maximum losses as **unlimited**.

The dangers for put options writers are also substantial. The writer of a put is obligated to pay the exercise price for assets that are delivered to him. Put options are only exercised when it is advantageous for the holder to do so. This will be when they can use the option to sell their assets at a higher price than would otherwise be available in the market.

To summarise, **options writers**, in return for receiving a premium, run very large risks. This is similar to the role undertaken by insurance companies. For a relatively modest premium, they are willing to insure your house against fire, but if your house burns down they will be faced with a claim for many thousands of pounds. The reasons why insurers and options writers enter into such contracts are that houses do not often burn down, and markets do not often rise or fall substantially. If writers price options properly they hope to make money in most instances. Option **writing** is not for the faint-hearted, nor for those without substantial resources. This said, many conservative users do write options as part of strategies involving the **holding** of the underlying asset. Such uses, which are known as **covered options**, are much less risky.

When investors buy or hold options, the risk is limited to the option's premium. If the market moves against them, they can simply decide not to exercise their options and sacrifice the premium. Remember, options holders have the right, **but not the obligation** to buy (call) or sell (put). If it does not make sense to buy or sell at the exercise price, the holder can decide to **abandon** the option and just lose the premium. Therefore, we can describe their maximum losses as **limited**.

3.3 Using options

3.3.1 Buying a call

This strategy is motivated by a view that an asset's price will rise (i.e. they are bullish).

Risk – the investor's risks are **limited to the premium** he pays for the options. So, if an 80p strike call option could be bought for a premium of 5p, this 5p is all he risks. The premium of the call option will only be a fraction of the cost of the underlying asset, so the option could first be considered less risky than buying the asset itself.

Whilst it is true that the monetary amount is relatively small, remember that the whole premium is at risk and it is easy to lose 100% of your investment, albeit a relatively small amount of money. Therefore, buying an option is considered to be riskier than buying the underlying shares.

Reward – the rewards from buying a call are **unlimited**. As the contract gives the holder the right to buy at a fixed price, this right will become increasingly valuable as the asset price rises above the exercise price. On the expiry date of the option, the profit made will be given by the amount by which the share price exceeds the exercise price less the premium paid.

Imagine an investor who buys one XYZ call option which gives him the right, but not the obligation, to buy the XYZ asset at a fixed price of 80p between now and the option's expiry date in January. The cost of this option is 5p.

If the asset price rises to 120p, the right to buy at 80p must be worth at least 40p. The net profit for the call would be 35p (40p – 5p). Of course, if the price of XYZ falls below 80p at the option's expiry date, the

80p call will be worthless and 100% of the initial 5p invested will be lost. This loss occurs because no sensible person would want the right to buy at 80p if they could buy the asset more cheaply elsewhere.

The buying of a call to **open** a position is known as a **long call**.

By using graphs, we can show how much an option will be worth at expiry. We offer them as an easier way to remember the maximum risks and rewards but do not worry if you find them hard to use.

Exam tip

> You will not be expected to create graphs in the exam, but they can help in understanding how options work.

On the vertical axis of the graph is profit/loss and on the horizontal axis is the asset price.

Long call: holder of 1 XYZ January 80p call   premium 5p

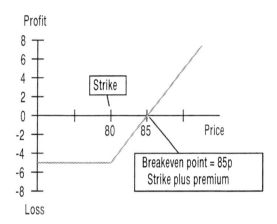

What the graph shows is that losses of 5p are made anywhere below 80p, whilst profits emerge above 85p. The amount of 85p represents the **breakeven point**. This is the point at which the original investment is recouped and it is calculated by simply adding the premium to the exercise price, e.g. 80p + 5p = 85p.

3.3.2 Selling a call

Risk – the selling (or writing) of a call, without at the same time being in possession of the underlying asset, is extremely risky. The risk is unlimited because the writer has a duty to deliver the asset at a fixed price regardless of the prevailing asset price. As the share price could, in theory, rise to infinity, the call writer assumes an **unlimited risk**. This strategy is sometimes called **naked** call writing and as it suggests, can leave you feeling very exposed.

Reward – you might ask why someone would assume such an unlimited risk. The answer, of course, is the hope of a profit. The **maximum profit** the writer can make is the **premium** he receives. Let us look again at an 80p call with a premium of 5p. The seller of this call will receive the 5p premium, and as long as the asset price at expiry is less than 80p, no one will rationally want to exercise the right to buy. The graph for selling a call is set out below. You will see that it is the equal and opposite of buying a call.

Short call: writer of 1 XYZ January 80p call   premium 5p

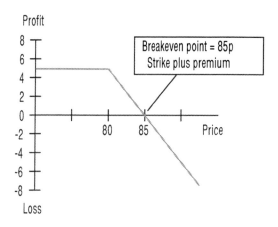

The selling of a call to open a position is known as a **short call**.

3.3.3 Buying a put

Risk – as when buying a call, the risk of buying a put is **limited to the premium paid**. The motivation behind buying a put will be to profit from a fall in the asset's price. The holder of a put obtains the right, but not the obligation, to **sell** at a fixed price. The value of this right will become increasingly valuable as the asset price falls.

Reward – the **greatest profit** that will arise from buying a put will be achieved if the **asset price falls to zero**.

Long put: holder of 1 XYZ January 80p put   premium 8p

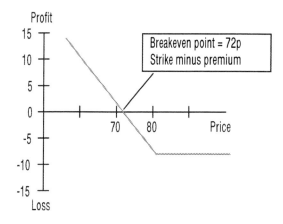

The **breakeven point**, and maximum profit, is calculated by deducting the premium from the exercise price, e.g. 80p – 8p = 72p. Like the purchase of a call, the premium needs to be recovered before profits are made. The buying of a put to open a position is known as a **long put**.

3.3.4 Selling a put

Risk – the selling of a put is dangerous as the writer enters into an obligation to purchase an asset at a fixed price. If the market price of that asset falls, the put writer will end up paying a large amount of money for what could be a valueless asset. The worst case will arise **when the asset price falls to zero. If this happens, the loss will be the exercise price less the premium received.**

Reward – what the put option writer hopes for is that the put will not be exercised. This will occur if the asset has a price above the exercise price at expiry. **The maximum reward is the premium received.** The selling of a put to open a position is known as a **short put**.

Short put: writer of 1 XYZ January 80p put   premium 8p

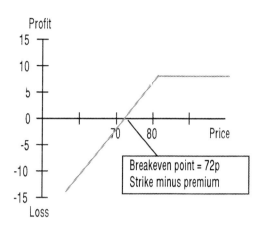

Exam tip	You will not be required to calculate the breakeven price in the exam.

4   RISKS SUMMARY: FUTURES AND OPTIONS

The table below summarises the risks and rewards from the basic speculative futures and options positions described in this chapter.

Position	Risk	Reward
Long Call	Limited to premium	Unlimited
Long Put	Limited to premium	Almost unlimited*
Short Call	Unlimited	Limited to premium
Short Put	Large but limited	Limited to premium
Long Future	Large but limited	Unlimited
Short Future	Unlimited	Large but limited

* Rewards are 'almost unlimited' – the price of the asset can only fall to zero.

5   INTEREST RATE SWAPS

An **interest rate swap** is an agreement to exchange, over an agreed period, two payment streams each calculated using a different type of interest rate, but which are based on the same notional principal amount. In a **vanilla IRS** a stream of floating rate payments is swapped for a stream of fixed rate payments.

Example

A company borrows £50m for 5 years at a variable rate (let's say LIBOR + 1%). They are concerned about rates rising so enter into a swap whereby they pay a fixed rate of 5.5% and receive LIBOR + 1%.

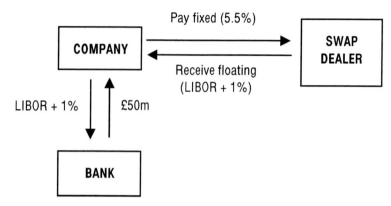

Remember that payments between the company and the swap dealer are netted off.

Results

1. LIBOR = 4%, company pays swap dealer 0.5%. Since they pay the bank 5% (LIBOR + 1%) in effect they are paying 5.5%.

2. LIBOR = 4.5%, no payment required to swap dealer. Company pays 5.5% to bank.

3. LIBOR = 5%, company receives 0.5% from swap dealer since they pay the bank 6% (LIBOR +1%) and receive 0.5% they are, in effect, paying 5.5%.

In each scenario, the company is 'locked in' at 5.5%.

CHAPTER ROUNDUP

- Derivatives – for example futures, options and swaps – derive their value from factors including movements in the price of an underlying asset. They can be used either for hedging risk or for speculation.

- Futures are tradable standardised contracts that allow a price to be agreed today for delivery of something at a future date.

- An option gives its holder a right, but not an obligation, to buy (call option) or to sell (put option) something. On the other side of the transaction is the writer of the option, who receives the premium from the option buyer, at the outset.

- An interest rate swap is an agreement to exchange, over an agreed period, two payment streams each calculated using a different type of interest rate, but which are based on the same notional principal amount.

TEST YOUR KNOWLEDGE

Check your knowledge of the Chapter here, without referring back to the text.

1.   What term is used for holding a position in order to reduce exposure to a risk?

2.   Someone buying a futures contract enters into an obligation to .... a .... quantity of a specified asset at a fixed future date, at a price agreed today. *[Fill in the blanks]*

3.   For whom are risks generally higher: call option holders or call option writers?

4.   Explain the difference between the premium and the strike price, in respect of options.

5.   John buys a call option from ABC Investment Bank for 20p that gives him the right to buy one share in XYZ plc for 450p. What is the maximum profit that ABC Investment Bank can realise on this trade?

6.   What is an interest rate swap?

TEST YOUR KNOWLEDGE: ANSWERS

1.   Hedging.

     See Section 1.1

2.   Someone buying a futures contract enters into an obligation to *buy* a *standardised* quantity of a specified asset at a fixed future date, at a price agreed today. The fact that the quantity is standardised is important to appreciate.

     See Section 2.1

3.   Call option writers bear potentially unlimited risks, since the rise in price of the asset is potentially unlimited. The maximum loss for the call option holder is the premium.

     See Section 3.2

4.   The premium is the cost of an option, which is paid by the holder and received by the writer. The exercise price or strike price is the price at which an options contract gives the right to buy (call) or sell (put) the asset.

     See Section 3.2

5.   The seller of an option charges a premium and this represents their maximum profit. Thus, in this case, the maximum profit is 20p.

     See Section 3.3.2

6.   An interest rate swap is an agreement to exchange, over an agreed period, two payment streams each calculated using a different type of interest rate, but which are based on the same notional principal amount.'

     See Section 5

4

Financial Products

Topics relating to financial products available to the ordinary 'retail' individual investor are examined in this chapter.

One of the functions of the financial sector is to intermediate between those who have funds to lend and those who wish to borrow. We outline the basics of deposit investments and of loans, including mortgage loans.

Various investment-related products have grown out of the life insurance sector, although there has recently been a shift towards more transparent investment products than many insurance-related products are. There has also been a move within the life sector from 'with profits' investment to 'unit-linked' products: these concepts are explained in this chapter

In the retirement planning field, pension schemes have been streamlined by the 'A'-Day changes that took place with effect from 6 April 2006.

CHAPTER CONTENTS

		Page
1	Deposits	76
2	Property	78
3	Pensions	79
4	Investment Bonds	82
5	Loans	83
6	Mortgages	85
7	Life Assurance	86
	Chapter Roundup	88
	Test Your Knowledge	89

CHAPTER LEARNING OBJECTIVES

Cash Deposits

- **Know** the characteristics of fixed term and instant access deposit accounts

- **Understand** the distinction between gross and net interest payments

- **Be able to calculate** the net interest due given the gross interest rate, the deposited sum, the period and tax rate

Property

- **Know** the characteristics of the property market

    - Commercial/residential property
    - Direct/indirect investment

- **Know** the advantages and disadvantages of investing in property

Pensions

- **Know** the tax incentives provided by pensions

- **Know** the basic characteristics of the following

    - State pension scheme

    - Occupational pension scheme

    - Personal pensions including self-invested personal pensions (SIPPs) and small self-administered schemes (SSASs)

    - Stakeholder pensions

Investment Bonds

- **Know** the tax incentives created by investment bonds – onshore/offshore

- **Know** the main characteristics of investment bonds

Loans

- **Know** the differences between bank loans, overdrafts and credit card borrowing

- **Know** the difference between the quoted interest rate on borrowing and the effective annual rate of borrowing

- **Be able to calculate** the effective annual rate of borrowing, given the quoted interest rate and frequency of payment

- **Know** the difference between secured and unsecured borrowing

Mortgages

- **Understand** the characteristics of the mortgage market:

  - Interest rates

- **Know** the definition of and types of mortgage:

  - Repayment
  - Interest only

Life Assurance

- **Know** the definition of the following types of life policy

  - Term assurance
  - Non-profit
  - With profits
  - Unit-linked policies

1 DEPOSITS

Know the characteristics of fixed term and instant access deposit accounts
Understand the distinction between gross and net interest payments
Be able to calculate the net interest due given the gross interest rate, the deposited sum, the period and tax rate

A **deposit** is a sum of money repayable on demand. This type of investment is seen as very low risk although inflation can reduce real return over time. Deposits offer investors good accessibility to their funds, with most deposit accounts offering either **instant access** or **three months' notice**.

It is likely that the rate of interest paid on a **fixed term account** is higher than that on an **easy access** basis, given that the investor will require compensation for the lower liquidity level.

Deposit accounts could be useful for short-term savings and 'rainy day' funds. Deposits also have the advantage of being an easily understandable investment.

From a **taxation** perspective interest is normally taxable at source at 20%, fulfilling the tax liability for a basic rate taxpayer. Higher rate taxpayers are subject to a further 20% on any interest earned. Banks and building societies are typical of the type of institutions that must normally deduct 20% tax on interest earned at source, and thus pay out only net interest.

A non-taxpayer can use HMRC form **R85** to give the deposit taker authority to pay interest **gross**, i.e. without deduction of tax.

Example: Deposits (1)

Mrs Smith is a higher rate taxpayer with a building society account that earns her £5,000 interest. She received however only £4,000 as interest income, which means that the building society has effectively taken off 20% tax (£1,000) on the gross amount earned at source. However, as a higher rate taxpayer, she has only paid half of her tax liability. In total, Mrs Smith owes 40% tax on the interest earned, £2,000 in total. Thus considering that £1,000 has already been paid at source, Mrs Smith has a further tax liability of £1,000, or the remaining 20% on the total gross amount earned.

Example: Deposits (2)

Mr Brown is a basic rate taxpayer who has received £200 building society interest. This amount is paid to Mr Brown net of 20% tax, which was deducted by the building society at source. The total amount of interest earned can be worked out given the rate of tax and the net amount received. It is simply a case of grossing up to adjust for the tax deducted at source.

£200 × 100/(100 − tax rate)

Thus   £200 × 100/80

= £250

Given that Mr Brown is a basic rate taxpayer, the tax deducted at source represents his total tax liability and thus there is no further amount owed to Her Majesty's Revenue and Customs (HMRC).

Further calculations may be performed given the interest rate, deposited sum, time period over which the investment is made and knowledge of the depositors marginal rate of tax.

Example: Deposit (3)

Mike Shaw is a basic rate taxpayer who deposits £7,200 in a bank account for five years. Mike will receive a simple rate of interest on the original deposit of 3.5%.

Gross interest earned would be = £7,200 × 3.5%

= £252 of interest per year

Thus, over five years £1,260 in interest is earned but this is a gross amount. To adjust for the 20% tax that Mike owes, we need to subtract 20% of this amount, which is £252 (£1,260 × 20%). Thus total net interest earned is £1,008 (£1,260 − £252) over the five-year period.

This could also be represented by the formula:

$$D_n = D_0 \times r \times n$$

where

D_n = is the amount at time n

D_0 = is the original amount deposited

r = the rate of interest

n = the time period

Then, to adjust for tax

Gross proceeds × (100 − tax rate)

where the tax rate is the tax applied at source, which is 20%

To calculate the amount of interest earned in any given year, we would simply use the formula:

$$i = D_0 \times r$$

which using the above example would be:

= £7,200 × 3.5%

= £252

Exam tip

The examiner will not require you to calculate the compounded interest.

2 PROPERTY

Know the characteristics of the property market: commercial/residential property; direct/indirect investment
Know the advantages and disadvantages of investing in property

2.1 Property

Property – land and buildings – is another form of investment, with certain special characteristics. Unlike stock exchange investments, property investments tend to be unique or **heterogeneous** in terms of location, design, condition and size. There may be a limited supply of properties available and in extreme cases the opportunity to buy property may be absolutely unique, such as the opportunity to acquire a historical building or property in a location of national interest.

Property is frequently **indivisible**, resulting in the cost of each individual, indivisible unit being significantly higher. As a result, property is often an unattainable investment medium for a small investor and hence they tend to invest indirectly by acquiring shares in property companies or through property bonds.

Unlike shares trading on a stock exchange, property is not sold on a central market. Property is normally bought and sold through agents in a particular location. The property market is said to be **decentralised**. To draw another parallel with securities, that can normally be sold when required, the property market may be highly **illiquid**.

Direct investment in property may involve **residential property** ('buy-to-let' investment) or **commercial property**. With both types of property, investors must take account of **void periods** between lettings, when no income is earned.

The major investors in commercial property are wealthy individuals and insurance company funds. The volatility in price of commercial property is lower than for equities. **Office** premises pay a higher return than **retail** (shops). **Industrial** property is a relativity expensive type of commercial property.

Investments in property are often financed through borrowings, with the lender having security over the property in case the borrower defaults. Investors will want to know the net yield they are achieving, from income less costs including borrowing costs. The rental yield is separate from any capital gain or loss from the value of the property rising or falling.

Advantages and disadvantages of investing in property

Advantages	Disadvantages
Potential capital growth	Difficulty of finding suitable tenants
Rental income	Value can decrease (as well as increase)
Can be less volatile than shares	Higher interest rates can affect the expected return
You can borrow someone's money (the bank's) and pay it back with someone else's money (the rental income)	Cost of repair/maintenance
	Legal requirements, e.g. safety certificates

3 PENSIONS

Know the tax incentives provided by pensions.
Know the basic characteristics of the state pension scheme, occupational pension schemes, personal pensions including SIPPs and SSASs, and stakeholder pensions.

3.1 Retirement planning

The purpose of pension provision is to provide an **income on retirement**. There **tax reliefs** attached to retirement savings made through contributions to registered pension schemes. We will examine four types of pension – the state pension scheme, occupational pension schemes, personal pensions and stakeholder pensions.

3.2 State pension

The UK government offers a **basic State-funded pension**. Those reaching the State Pension Age from 6 April 2010 onwards receive the full level of the basic State pension if they have 30 qualifying years, generally through their national insurance contributions record. Those with fewer qualifying years will receive one thirtieth of the full amount for each qualifying year. A couple receives a higher rate of basic State pension than a single person.

The State Pension Age is 65 for men is 65 and 60 for women, but equalisation to age 65 will be phased in from 2010 through to 2020. State Pension age will increase for both men and women from age 65 to 68 between 2024 and 2046.

In addition to the basic State pension, there is a **State Second Pension (S2P)**. The level of this pension is linked to the earnings of the individual whilst they were at work. It is only paid to employees, not those who are self-employed.

Both the basic State pension and pensions paid under S2P are paid gross but are taxable.

3.3 Occupational pension schemes (OPS)

There are two main types of occupational (work-based) pension schemes:

- The defined benefit (also known as final salary) schemes
- Defined contribution (also known as money purchase) schemes

3.3.1 Defined benefit – final salary

Typically the maximum occupational pension for most people in a defined scheme will be two thirds of final salary after 40 years of service. With final salary (defined benefit) schemes, the pension paid on retirement is related to the **service of the individual** with the company, e.g. 1/60th of the final pay. Tax relief is offered for both the employer and employee on contributions into occupational schemes.

The benefit that is paid on retirement is guaranteed and thus is very attractive to the employee. It is possible to increase the benefit paid on retirement by contributing into an Additional Voluntary Contribution (AVC) scheme provided by the employer ('in-house') or by an external provider.

In recent years, most final salary schemes have been closed to a new employees of a firm, leaving them with a choice between money purchase schemes or having all contributions paid into a type of personal pension plan. The cost of meeting the funding requirements of defined salary schemes has become extremely high in recent years, hence the unwillingness of employers to continue providing them.

3.3.2 Defined contribution – money purchase

Money purchase schemes are also provided by employers but the pension provided on retirement is not normally linked to final remuneration. The employer pays a set amount of money into the fund (i.e. defined contribution), with the value of the fund at retirement being used to purchase an annuity. The level of pension that will be provided therefore is linked not only to the value of the fund but the annuity rate at retirement. The risk of such a scheme is with the employee as there is **no link with final remuneration**.

3.4 Personal pensions

Personal Pension Plans (PPs) are typically individual arrangements to provide for a pension on retirement, although **group** personal pensions may be offered by an employer who does not have an occupational scheme. PPs are generally **money purchase schemes**.

As with other registered pension schemes, the normal minimum age for taking benefits is 50, until 5 April 2010, after which the minimum age will increase to 55. Income, within given limits, can be drawn down from the fund after this age but, by age 75, an annuity must normally be purchased using the fund remaining.

A **tax-free cash lump sum of 25%** of the fund can be taken when income benefits start.

If the tax-free cash lump sum is taken there will be less money in the fund to pay for income 'drawdown' or to buy an annuity and thus the pension will be lower.

3.4.1 Self-invested personal pension (SIPP)

With a **Self Invested Personal Pension (SIPP)**, as its name implies, the individual can decide which investments to buy.

3.4.2 Small self-administered schemes

Small Self Administered Schemes (SSASs) are OPSs used by small companies (often family owned) and can have no more than 11 members, one of whom must be a controlling director.

The fund can borrow money, i.e. gear up, and often buy property then rent it to the company at prevailing market rates.

Members benefit by buying annuities or drawing income from the fund.

3.5 Stakeholder pensions

Stakeholder pension plans (SHPs) were introduced in April 2001 and follow similar rules to personal pension plans, except that the following rules or '**CAT** standards' apply to SHPs.

- **C**harges. For new plans, charges are limited to 1.5% of the fund value p.a. for the first ten years and 1% p.a. thereafter. For plans started before April 2005, a limit of 1% applies in all years.

- **A**ccess. The minimum contribution level must not exceed £20.

- **T**erms. Contributions can be raised or stopped without penalty. Transfers in or out attract no exit penalty.

3.6 Post-April 2006 pension regime

A new UK pension regime was introduced on 6 April 2006, the date known as 'A-day'.

The new 'simplified' regime covers all types of pension arrangement, including occupational as well as personal and stakeholder schemes.

The new scheme is based on allowances rather than absolute limits. if the allowances are exceeded, there are tax penalties which make this unattractive.

- The **lifetime allowance** puts a limit on the total amount of benefit that can be accumulated under tax-advantaged pension schemes by a single individual. The lifetime allowance is tested as benefits crystallise (for example, on retirement), and is set at £1,800,000 for the years 2010/11 to 2015/16. Those with large funds already in place at 6 April 2006 can apply to have their value 'protected' from the lifetime provision.

- The **annual allowance** puts overall limits on the amount of contributions, or the increase in benefits in the case of defined benefit schemes, which can receive tax advantages for a single individual. The allowance is tested each year and its level is £255,000 for 2010/11 to 2015/16. See below on how this allowance is applied.

3.7 Tax reliefs for pension schemes

ning objective **Know** the tax incentives provided by pensions.

Registration of a pension scheme with HMRC means that the following tax reliefs will apply.

- Contributions by individuals will enjoy tax relief – normally at the individual's highest tax rate, but new rules are currently proposed to be introduced for those with incomes of at least £150,000 (see below)

- Employers' contributions will be deducted from the business profits for tax purposes.

- The pension fund's investment return is free of tax on income and gains, although dividend tax credits cannot be reclaimed.

- Part of the retirement benefits can be taken as a tax-free lump sum (25% of the fund for a defined contribution scheme, or an equivalent amount based on a commutation factor for a defined benefit scheme).

Those earning an adjusted income of at least £150,000 could be affected by new rules introduced in the 2009 Budget. It is proposed that higher rate tax relief will be tapered away for those earning between £150,000 and £180,000 from 6 April 2011 and, from that date, those with incomes above £180,000 will receive only basic rate relief. To avoid people pre-empting these rules, a special 20% charge applies in 2010/11 to contributions that are more than £20,000 in excess of the individual's normal established pattern of contributions.

Note that income drawn from the pension scheme is taxable. Therefore, except for the 25% lump-sum that is received tax free when benefits are taken, a pension scheme generally provides **deferral** of tax. This deferral of tax means that pension schemes can be an advantageous savings vehicles for those who get higher rate tax relief while they are contributing to the scheme, but expect to pay basic rate tax when they draw pension benefits later. Against this factor must be weighed the relative inflexibility of the schemes when it comes to drawing benefits: the requirement to buy an annuity by age 75 is seen by some as being restrictive. **Individual Savings Accounts (ISAs)** (covered in Chapter 6) can be considered as a more flexible alternative tax-advantaged savings vehicle.

3.8 Eligibility

Under HMRC rules, most people under the age of 75 are now eligible to be a member of a registered pension scheme. Individuals can contribute to, and build up benefits in, as many registered schemes as they want, and can accrue benefits under both occupational and personal schemes **at the same time** (this has been restricted, previously).

An individual will be eligible provided that he:

- Has **UK earnings** (from either employment or self-employment) chargeable to income tax in the tax year, or

- Is **resident** in the UK at some time in the tax year, or

- Was resident in the UK during the **five tax years** immediately preceding that tax year, **and** started the scheme while he was a UK-resident, or

- Has earnings from **overseas Crown employment** subject to UK tax in that year or is the spouse or civil partner of someone who has.

3.9 Member contributions

Gross pension contributions for individuals qualifying for tax relief are limited to the higher £3,600 per year and 100% of earnings, subject to the overriding limit of the annual allowance.

4 INVESTMENT BONDS

Learning objectives   **Know** the tax incentives created by investment bonds – onshore/offshore
Know the main characteristics of investment bonds

4.1 Features of investment bonds

An investment bond is a life insurance designed to provide growth or income, or a combination of both, on a single lump sum investment. Sometimes these products are called Single Premium Life Assurance Bonds. When you invest, your money is placed into one or more investment funds of the investor's choice with each fund divided into units. These funds might invest in the various asset classes: equity, fixed income, property, cash. With each unit individually priced, the investor can calculate the value of the bond by multiplying the 'unit price' by the number of units held.

The normal minimum investment is £5,000 and the investment is usually regarded as medium term (5 years) or long term (10 or more years). The bond will normally pay out 101% of the fund value at the time of death.

Investors are able to withdraw 5% of the total payment made without any immediate tax liability each year. These withdrawals are taken into account when the bond is encashed.

Since the fund pays tax at 20% on investment income there is no further tax liability for basic rate tax payers. However, higher rate taxpayers will be liable to a further 20% on the chargeable gain.

4.2 Offshore investment bonds

Features of **offshore bonds** are as follows.

- UK life offices with offshore subsidiaries, such as Standard Life and Scottish Widows, issue insurance bonds from their offices in the Channel Islands, Isle of Man, Dublin and Luxembourg.

- The advantage of the offshore bond is that the underlying life funds suffer little or no tax (gross roll up) compared with UK life funds which are taxed at 20%. This tax situation may be advantageous for UK higher rate taxpayers.

- However, the costs of offshore products are typically higher than onshore because the insurance company is unable to offset expenditure against income for tax purposes. A typical charging structure could be 6% initial charge with 1.5% annual management charge.

- An offshore bond should be maintained for as long a period as possible. Because of the charges, it can take five years for the value of the offshore fund to start to edge ahead of the UK fund for a basic rate taxpayer, and longer for a higher rate taxpayer.

- Withdrawals of up to 5% of the original investment may be taken for 20 years without an immediate tax liability. If the 5% allowance is not used in one year, it can be carried forward to the next.

- A non-taxpayer might use an offshore bond. In this case money could roll up in a virtually tax-free fund and on encashment any chargeable gain will not be subject to tax. However this may not be a worthwhile exercise because the high charges imposed on the bond may wipe out the tax advantage.

5 LOANS

5.1 Introduction

There are times when private investors can spend more that they earn by financing this extra expenditure through a variety of short-term borrowing instruments, which include bank loans, overdraft facilities and credit cards. Perhaps the most common form of borrowing by private investors is through **bank loans**. This is where an individual will apply to borrow a particular sum of money from a bank for a given period of time at a particular rate of interest. The individual must make repayments on the loan according to a prescribed schedule. This allows an investor to spread the repayments over a more manageable timescale

Overdrafts may be used to provide individuals with extra money in the short term too. The individual will again agree a limit of the facility with the bank known as the overdraft limit, which represents ready money to allow the individual to spend beyond the current funds available in the account. Repayment terms and periods are normally tailor-made to suit the individual's needs and any amount up to the agreed limit may be drawn upon.

Credit card companies provide an additional facility for individuals again wishing to make purchases in excess of their current account balances. Credit card companies will assess the creditworthiness of an individual in order to establish a credit limit against which payments can be made. From the other side, credit cards provide retail clients a flexible form of unsecured, short-term financing at relatively high rates of interest.

As far as interest charges are concerned, the bank or credit card company will normally quote both a rate of interest as well as an annual equivalent rate. We will now examine the differences between each of these briefly.

The rate of interest charged on a loan will vary according to the level of **base rates** and if you are taking a repayment loan, the length of time over which you are planning to repay the loan.

The interest rate paid can be calculated in several different ways. The norm in **mortgage** lending is for interest to be calculated annually as a percentage of the outstanding capital balance. There are, however, mortgages where the interest is calculated on a daily basis.

Therefore, interest rates on mortgages, **personal loans**, savings accounts and credit cards will all in turn usually be linked directly or indirectly to base rates.

Personal loans, credit cards, mortgages and overdrafts may all be quoted at introductory rates of interest that sound very cheap. However, what introductory rates fail to include are any arrangement fees you may be charged for loans and they also will not immediately reflect any higher rate of interest that your borrowings will ultimately revert to.

The **Annual Equivalent Rate (AER)** which effectively amounts to the same thing as the **Annual Percentage Rate (APR)**, is a useful standardised guide to the rate someone will actually pay. The method of calculating the APR is specified by the Financial Services Authority. The difference is that 'AER' applies to products which may be in credit or debit, while 'APR' is the measure quoted for pure lending products.

5.2 Annual equivalent rate

Learning objective	**Be able to calculate** the effective annual rate of borrowing, given the quoted interest rate and frequency of payment

Annual Equivalent Rate (AER) is a notional rate that is quoted on loans. It will demonstrate what the interest paid would be if the interest was **compounded and paid annually instead of monthly** (or any other period). If an interest is paid more than once a year (monthly or quarterly, for example) then the AER is calculated by deducting each interest payment from the loan and then calculating the next interest payment, compounding the interest. Thus, on accounts where interest is paid quarterly, the AER will be slightly higher than the quoted gross rate because of the compound interest on the interest paid during the year.

Example: AER

Mr Jones borrows £500 from the bank. Interest charges are quoted at 12% p.a., paid quarterly.

At the end of the first quarter, the interest is due on the original amount borrowed.

$$£500 \times 3\% = £15$$

By the end of the second quarter, the interest is due on the original amount borrowed plus the first quarter interest.

$$£515 \times 3\% = £15.45$$

The same process now applies to the interest charged at the end of the third quarter.

$$£530.45 \times 3\% = £15.91$$

And the fourth quarter

$$£546.36 \times 3\% = £16.39$$

The quoted rate is 12% p.a. However, the AER is calculated as follows.

$$(1+r_1)\times(1+r_2)\times(1+r_3)\times(1+r_4) = 1+\text{AER}$$

Thus

$$\text{AER} = \left[(1+0.03)\times(1+0.03)\times(1+0.03)\times(1+0.03)\right]-1$$
$$= \left[1.03\times1.03\times1.03\times1.03\right]-1$$
$$= 1.1255-1$$
$$= 0.1255 = 12.55\%$$

5.3 Secured and unsecured borrowing

Know the difference between secured and unsecured borrowing

Finally, we turn our attention to the terms **secured borrowing** and **unsecured borrowing**. If a bank requests security on a loan, this is normally done to reduce the risk faced by the bank. An example would be a mortgage agreement, where if the borrower does not keep up with repayments on the mortgage, the bank has the right to seize the asset attached as security on the loan, i.e. the house. When there is a secured charge over an asset in a loan agreement, the rate of interest charged will usually be lower than when no security is requested. This is due to the fact that an asset may be seized in the event of default and hence the risk profile for the lender is lowered.

On the other hand, where no security is provided for, for example with credit cards, the rate of interest charges will be much higher. This is because the borrower now represents a much higher risk to the lending institution and thus they will try and recoup as much of the loan as possible through high repayments. If the borrower did indeed default, then the lender could well have achieved a sizeable portion of repayment by that time and hence cover some of the outstanding position.

6 MORTGAGES

Know the definition of and types of mortgage; repayment mortgages; interest only mortgages

A mortgage is defined as 'a conveyance of land or an assignment of chattels as security for the payment of a debt or some other obligation for which it is given'. In everyday language, a mortgage is taken to mean the **loan** that is used to **purchase a property**, with the loan secured against the property by the lender.

The market for mortgages is very competitive but traditional providers such as banks and building societies have maintained their market dominance in this area.

6.1 Repayment mortgages

With a repayment mortgage, payment is **part interest** and **part capital**. At the outset of the loan the repayment is mainly interest but as the term progresses, the capital element becomes a bigger part of the monthly repayment. If full payments are made on time then the loan will be repaid at the end of the term. There is normally a choice of terms and types of interest rate associated with these products and they are easy for borrowers to understand. However, should general interest rates rise, then borrowers face heavier repayments and if they are unable to meet these additional amounts, their homes would be at risk. Repayment mortgages normally require **bigger monthly repayments** than interest only mortgages.

6.2 Interest only mortgages

With an interest only mortgage, the monthly payment is interest only. There is no payment towards the capital element. Therefore, at the end of the term, the whole amount of the capital element is still outstanding. An alternative savings vehicle may be used to make the capital repayment. An example here would be a pension-linked mortgage where the tax-free cash lump sum of 25% can be used to pay off the capital.

6.3 Mortgage interest rates

With mortgages, various interest rate arrangements can apply.

6.3.1 Variable rate

This is when the rate charged by the mortgage lender **varies** according to a **prescribed formula**. Thus when general interest rates rise, monthly repayments will rise in line with this increase and likewise fall, as general interest rates fall too. While a loan arrangement with this type of interest charge does not afford absolute certainty as to the monthly prepayments, it does allow lenders to benefit in times of a lower interest rate climate.

6.3.2 Fixed rate

The interest rate may be **fixed for a certain period** and then it will **revert to a variable rate**. This is advantageous for those homeowners wishing to lock in a degree of certainty for a particular period of time. Fixed rates over the entire length of the mortgage arrangement are common in European mortgage markets but are far less common in the UK market, which leads to many homeowners remortgaging their properties every couple of years as the term of their fixed rate expires.

6.3.3 Capped rate

This is a **maximum limit** on the loan interest rate, which would be advantageous in times of constant interest rate rises. The borrower would only ever face increased payments as interest rates rose up to a certain level.

6.3.4 Discounted rate

There is a genuine **reduction on the interest** for an **initial period**, which is usually aimed at attracting first-time buyers. Some mortgage providers offer an interest rate that tracks the Bank of England base rate (known as a tracker rate), with an additional discount applied to this rate.

7   LIFE ASSURANCE

Life assurance policies provide **protection against death** and will pay out a capital sum on maturity of the policy or surrender. The purpose of life insurance is to provide payment to beneficiaries upon the death of the life assured (the person whose death leads to a payout on the policy). The life assured does not necessarily have to be the same person as the policyholder. In order to take out a life policy on someone else, the proposer would have to show an insurable interest (i.e. prove financial loss on the death of the life assured). It is also possible to take out joint life policies.

- **Term assurance** – the policy covers the life assured against the risk of death during a **specified term**, with the payout only if death should occur during that term. There is no surrender or maturity value on the policy. It is viewed as the **cheapest** form of life cover, as the sum assured remains constant throughout the specified term. It is often used to cover fixed term loans and interest-only mortgages where life cover is not provided with the repayment vehicle.

  With term assurance, it is common for the life cover to be written on one of the three following bases.

  - **Level** – the amount of cover remains throughout the term of the policy. This would be used in the case of an interest-only mortgage where life cover is required.

  - **Decreasing** – the amount of life cover decreases throughout the term of the policy. This would be used for a repayment mortgage – as the amount of capital owed reduces, the level of life cover required can reduce also.

  - **Increasing** – cover may increase over the term of the policy. This may be used where the life assured wishes to protect the value of their life cover against increases in inflation.

- **Whole of life assurance** and **endowment policies** are guaranteed to pay out:

  - On death for whole of life, and
  - On death or policy expiry for endowments

There are a number of types of whole life and endowment policies. Some policies are termed **non-profit policies**. These policies have a guaranteed sum assured only, which is paid whenever death occurs or when the endowment term ends. Premiums on these policies normally remain constant but may cease at a certain age.

With-profit policies also have a guaranteed sum assured on death but, in addition, there will be an added reversionary bonus and possibly a terminal bonus. Premiums will be higher than for a non-profit policy. The return on these policies is linked to the value of the life fund. With-profits policies are a cautious risk investment, designed to 'smooth' the returns from underlying investments through the bonus system.

Unit-linked policies have a direct link with the performance of the underlying fund, and normally there is a wide choice of funds available to invest in, with many funds allowing switching between units. The investor pays monthly premiums, which are used to buy units within a fund. The usual bid-offer spread will apply, which for these products is normally about 5%. In addition to the spread, there is an annual management charge of about 0.75% to 1%. As with most types of investment, the value of the units may fluctuate and thus the amount paid out is not certain. Policies may have two types of unit, initial and accumulation. These tend to be 10-year policies. On surrender the bid value of the units is paid to the holder.

CHAPTER ROUNDUP

- Deposits are easily understood by investors and can offer liquidity (accessibility) as well as security of capital.

- Direct investments in property (land and buildings) tend to be heterogeneous and are often indivisible.

- Pension scheme offer a tax –incentivised way of providing an income in retirement.

- State pension arrangements include a basic pension with entitlement based on national insurance contributions, and an earnings-related State Second Pension (S2P).

- Work-based (occupational) pension schemes may be either defined benefit ('final salary') or defined contribution ('money purchase').

- A stakeholder pension scheme follows similar rules to personal pension plans except that there is a cap on charges.

- Investment bonds have a life assurance component but are mainly used for investment purposes.

- Loans may be secured (e.g. mortgages) or unsecured (e.g. credit cards). The Annual Percentage Rate is a standardised measure of the annual interest payable.

- A mortgage is a loan secured against property by the lender.

- Life assurance ranges from term polices, which pay out on death within a term, to more investment-related policies such as endowment policies, which pay out a sum on death or on survival until maturity of the policy.

TEST YOUR KNOWLEDGE

Check your knowledge of the Chapter here, without referring back to the text.

1. Maria opens an instant access account which pays 4.5% annual interest gross. She makes an opening deposit of £6,450 and makes no further deposits or withdrawals. After 7 months, Maria closes the account and the bank pays her the full interest due after deducting 20% tax. How much does Maria receive on closure (principal *plus* interest)? (Account for the interest on a monthly basis.)

2. Gerald is a non-taxpayer who has received £738 in bank deposit interest net, after deduction of 20% tax. How much tax can he reclaim?

3. Typically, a direct investment in property cannot easily be realised quickly. This can best be explained by saying that property is generally:

    A   Heterogeneous
    B   Illiquid
    C   Indivisible
    D   Expensive

4. What is the maximum annual management charge for a new stakeholder pension plan?

    A   0.5%
    B   1.0%
    C   1.5%
    D   2.0%

5. The AER for a loan is the rate of interest calculated on the assumption that the interest is compounded and paid:

    A   Annually
    B   Monthly
    C   Quarterly
    D   Daily

6. A borrower who wants to get the best advantage from sharply falling interest rates should probably choose:

    A   A capped rate mortgage
    B   A fixed rate mortgage
    C   A variable rate mortgage
    D   An endowment mortgage

7. Mr and Mrs Hoover are taking out a 10-year repayment mortgage and want the mortgage to be paid off in full if either of them were to die. What type of policy is likely to be most suitable and offer the best value?

    A   Whole of life assurance
    B   Level term assurance
    C   Decreasing term assurance
    D   Increasing term assurance

TEST YOUR KNOWLEDGE: ANSWERS

1. £6,450 × 4.5% × 0.8 × 7/12 = £135.45

    £6,450 + £135.45 = **£6,585.45** – the amount Maria will receive.

    See Section 1

2. £738 × 100/80 = £922.50 gross interest

    Tax to reclaim: £922.50 – £738.00 = **£184.50**.

    See Section 1

3. The fact that a buyer might not be found quickly for a property is a reflection of the illiquidity of property, and so B is the best answer.

    See Section 2.1

4. C is the correct answer.

    See Section 3.5

5. A is the correct answer. The Annual Equivalent Rate (AER) demonstrates what the interest paid would be if the interest were compounded and paid annually instead of monthly or over any other period.

    See Section 5.2

6. With a variable rate mortgage, general falls in interest rates should be reflected in reductions in the variable rate, and so C is the best answer.

    See Section 6.3

7. C is the best answer. A decreasing term policy can pay off the remaining principal, which will decrease over the mortgage term. Whole of life assurance is not limited to a specified term and would typically be much more expensive than a term policy.

    See Section 7

5

Pooled Investment Funds

Most ordinary investors cannot easily gain exposure to a number of different shares or different sectors conveniently and without incurring relatively high costs. The sectors of financial services industry that offer 'pooled' investment products can help.

In the UK, the main types of pooled investment are unit trusts, open ended investment companies, investment trusts and exchange-traded funds. In this chapter, we explain each of these types of fund in turn.

We also look briefly at hedge funds, which may be used by more sophisticated investors with relatively large amounts to invest.

We will also look at a relatively new type of pooled investment called Real Estate Investment Trusts (REITs).

CHAPTER CONTENTS

Page

1   Collective Investment 94
2   Unit Trusts..95
3   Open-Ended Investment Companies (OEICs) 99
4   Investment Trusts 101
5   Exchange-Traded Funds...103
6   Hedge Funds 103
7   Real Estate Investment Trusts (REITs) 104
Chapter Roundup...105
Test Your Knowledge 107

CHAPTER LEARNING OBJECTIVES

Introduction

- **Understand** the benefits of collective investment
- **Understand** the scope and range of investment strategies – active v passive
- **Know** the differences between authorised and unauthorised funds
- **Know** the purpose and principal features of UCITS
- **Know** the differences between onshore and offshore funds

Unit Trusts

- **Know** the definition of a unit trust
- **Know** the types of authorised unit trusts available
- **Know** the roles of the Manager and the Trustee

Open-Ended Investment Companies (OEICs)

- **Know** the definition and legal structure of an OEIC
- **Know** the roles of the Authorised Corporate Director and the Depositary
- **Know** the terms ICVC, SICAV and the context in which they are used

Pricing, Dealing and Settling

- **Know** how unit trusts and OEIC shares are priced
- **Know** the ways in which charges can be made by the fund manager
- **Know** how shares and units are bought and sold
- **Know** how collectives are settled

Investment Trusts

- **Know** the characteristics of an investment trust

    - Share classes
    - Gearing

- **Understand** the factors that affect the price of an investment trust
- **Know** the meaning of the discounts and premiums in relation to investment trusts
- **Know** how investment trust shares are traded

Real Estate Investment Trusts (REITs)

- **Know** the basic characteristics of REITs

    - Tax efficient
    - Property diversification
    - Liquidity
    - Risk

Exchange-Traded Funds

- **Know** the main characteristics of Exchange-Traded Funds
- **Know** how Exchange-Traded Funds are traded

Hedge Funds

- **Know** the basic characteristics of hedge funds

    - Risks and risk types
    - Cost and liquidity
    - Investment strategies

1   COLLECTIVE INVESTMENT

Understand the benefits of collective investment

Understand the scope and range of investment strategies – active v passive

1.1 Features and benefits of collective investment

As we have seen, there are wide ranges of instruments in which an individual can invest his surplus money. In order to minimise the risk involved in investment it is important to spread such funds over a range of instruments, thereby diversifying risk. However, if the individual has a limited amount of money to invest, it will be prohibitively expensive to do this. For example, if the sum available is only £3,000, it will be very difficult to buy a sufficiently wide range of investments. This will mean exposure to a small number of holdings and therefore a concentration of risk. In other words, putting all your eggs in one basket.

One way around this problem is for individuals to be grouped together and form a collective investment vehicle. Here they pool their money in a large fund, which is managed and invested for them by a fund manager.

There are several types of collective investment vehicle available, the main types being **unit trusts**, **open-ended investment companies (OEICs)** and **investment trusts**.

Authorised unit trusts and OEICs are **Authorised Investment Funds (AIFs)** and often referred to simply as **funds**.

A unit trust differs from investment trusts and OEICs in the way it is set up, as a unit trust is not a company with shares. Another key difference between a unit trust and a investment trust is the way in which the fund prices itself. For unit trusts, there is a direct relationship between the value of the underlying investments and the value of units. We say that unit trusts are priced according to Net Asset Value (NAV). Investment trust shares, however, are priced according to supply and demand in the stock market.

1.2 Passive v active investment strategies

A collective fund may be managed actively or passively.

- The **active** fund manager will analyse the investments and sectors in which a fund invests, and will base decisions about whether to buy or sell on this analysis.

- With **passive** index-tracking fund management, the criterion for inclusion of a particular stock in the fund portfolio is simply that a share forms part of the index.

Index tracking involves investing in the shares that make up the index, in the proportions in which those shares make up the index. An **index tracker fund** aims to match the performance of a particular index, such as the FTSE 100 Share Index, thus giving the investor an opportunity to benefit from positive movements in the overall market.

A tracker will not generally be able to match the total return (including dividends) from an **index** consistently, because of:

- Variations arising from **tracking errors** (see below)

- **Transaction costs** arising from buying and selling the shares held in the fund (spread and dealing commission)

- **Charges** levied by the manager of the tracker, to cover the manager's costs and profit

Management costs for tracker funds should be relatively low. The fund only requires **passive management** because there is no need for research to be undertaken as with an **actively managed** fund.

Tracker funds can occur in various forms, including unit trusts, OEICs/ICVCs, investment trusts and exchange traded funds (ETFs). We discuss these types of collective investment below.

2 UNIT TRUSTS

Know the definition of a unit trust
Know the roles of the Manager and Trustee
Know the differences between authorised and unauthorised funds
Know how unit trusts are priced
Know the ways in which charges can be made by the fund manager
Know how units are bought and sold
Know how collectives are settled

2.1 The nature of a unit trust

A **unit trust** is a legal trust. Under its terms, individuals pool their money, which is then invested by the trustees with a fund manager who manages the money. The funds relating to the trust are held in a trust fund, which is run in accordance with the rules laid down in the trust deed.

The assets of the trust are legally owned by a **trustee** on behalf of beneficiaries, who are known as the unit holders. The trustee of a unit trust tends to be a bank or insurance company.

A **fund manager** (who runs the fund and makes the day-to-day investment management decisions) appoints the trustee. The job of the trustee is to protect the investor's interests by ensuring that the manager adheres to the rules and regulations that are stipulated in the trust deed. Therefore, we have seen that there are two parties to a unit trust, the manager and the trustee. To prevent conflicts of interest, it is necessary that the manager and the trustee are independent of each other.

As we will see later in this section, all trading takes place through fund managers, and if an individual wishes to add money to the fund he will receive a receipt in return, referred to as a unit in the fund. The fund manager makes a market in these units and may well have second-hand or redeemed units which he can sell to new investors (known as **box management**). Unit trusts in the UK are, like OEICs (discussed below), called **open-ended** funds as there is no limit to the amount of money which can be invested. If no second-hand units are available, the fund is permitted to create more units and expand the fund.

2.2 Authorisation

Some unit trusts are authorised by the Financial Services Authority (FSA) and acquire the status '**authorised**'. Only regulated unit trusts may be freely marketed to the public. Once a trust is authorised, it must abide by the FSA rules. These rules limit both the types of investment that can be entered into within a specific trust and the amounts of those investments compared to the size of the fund.

The rules and regulations are designed to ensure that the investors take a limited amount of risk. Should an investor wish to take more risk within the auspices of a collective investment scheme, there are a number of alternative authorised funds, which provide a range of risk profiles.

The FSA also requires a formal trust deed to be established which again will place limits on the powers of the trustees and the fund managers. Normally, unit trusts specify the nature of the investments into which they will enter, for example, Korean Equities. The trust deed will also cover administrative matters such as the fees the fund manager is able to take from the fund each year, and the precise method of calculating the bid and offer prices at which units will be traded.

2.3 Types of authorised fund

Know the types of authorised unit trusts available

As discussed, **authorised unit trusts** can be freely marketed to the general public.

In order to apply for authorisation, a **fund** (which includes both unit trusts and Open Ended Investment Companies – covered below) must be proposed as one of the following types.

- A **UCITS scheme**
- A **non-UCITS retail scheme (NURS)**
- A **qualified investor scheme (QIS)**

UCITS schemes must comply with the conditions of the European UCITS Directive, which we discuss later in this Section.

As the name implies, a **NURS** is a scheme that does not comply with all of the UCITS conditions. In practice, there are relatively few NURSs.

A **QIS** is a type of scheme that may only be promoted to professional investors on the same terms as an unregulated collective investment scheme. A QIS needs to obtain FSA approval in order to become a non-UCITS retail scheme (NURS).

2.3.1 Unregulated funds

The marketing rules for unregulated unit trusts are much more restrictive in that it is forbidden to promote these trusts to private investors, limiting the market solely to professionals. Often these unregulated higher risk funds are referred to as **hedge funds**, which we discuss later in this Chapter.

2.4 Charges

The **charges** on a unit trust must be explicit in the trust deed and documentation. They should give details of the current charges and the extent to which managers can change them. These charges can be taken in one or more of three ways, via an **initial charge**, an **exit charge** or through **annual management charges**.

The **initial charge** is added to the **buying price**. So, the buyer suffers both the bid/offer spread, and the initial charge. Managers might charge 3.0-6.5% on **equities**, and less on **fixed interest funds** (1-4%). Other funds with lower charges include **index tracker funds** and **cash/money market funds**, where the lower price reflects the lower burden of management. Where an initial charge is small or non-existent, there may be a further charge on exit.

As an alternative to initial charges, a few trusts apply **exit charges**. These charges are typically invoked where the investor sells the investment within a set period of time, e.g. five years. Funds that make such a charge are indicated by an **E** in the *Financial Times*.

An **annual charge** of around 0.5–1.5% of the underlying fund will generally be made to cover the ongoing cost of the investment management of the trust. In some cases, part of the annual management charge is paid to intermediaries as **renewal commission**, typically at a rate of 0.5% per annum. **Tracker funds** require less management and costs will be **lower**.

FSA rules permit **performance-related charges**. These may be based on growth of the fund, or out-performance of the fund's standard benchmark. The basis of the charges must be disclosed in the fund prospectus and key features document.

2.5 Buying, selling and settlement of units

There is **no secondary market** in the units themselves. An individual can only buy or sell units directly with the **fund manager** or **through an intermediary**, such as an independent financial adviser (IFA). The price of units is based on the asset value of the fund. For example, if the fund has assets under management of £200m and there are 100m units in issue, each unit has a value of £2.00.

However, the fund manager will be able to make a spread (i.e. the difference between bid and offer) around that price. The spread allows the fund manager to be compensated for costs incurred in dealing with the fund, such as stamp duty and other dealing fees, as well as to make a profit. The ability to set two different prices, one for buying (bid) and one for selling (offer), is known as **dual pricing.**

2.6 Bid and offer basis

Pricing of unit trusts begins with the **creation price**, which is the price the manager must pay to the trustee in order to create a new unit. It is a reflection of the value of the underlying investments the fund manager has made, based upon the valuation at a particular time of the day. Creation of units must take place within 2 hours of the valuation point.

For example, in pricing the unit above, using a (large) spread of 15% would allow a spread of £1.85 to £2.15. When there are many investors selling the units of the fund, it is likely that the manager of the unit trust will price around the cancellation price (the lowest price). This is sometimes known as the **bid basis.** The bid basis might be £1.85 to £2.00. Operating on a bid basis encourages new money to come into the fund, and discourages money from leaving the fund.

If it is likely that lots of investors want to buy into the fund, the manager will price around the creation price (the highest price). This is sometimes known as the **offer basis**, say, £2.00 to £2.15.

Whilst the fund manager may operate at any point within that spread range, the **cancellation price** must be available on request. The cancellation price will be at the bottom end of the range, which in this case is £1.85.

When an investor wishes to exit the fund and sell his units, the fund manager may either cancel his holding or keep the units, placing them instead in a box. These units can then be reissued to a new investor, thus eliminating the need to create new additional units for investors buying into the fund **(box management)**.

2.7 Recognised overseas schemes

Know the differences between onshore and offshore funds

Overseas schemes may be generally marketed in the UK, provided they are recognised by the FSA. **Recognition** will be granted where the FSA is satisfied as to the local regulatory control in the country in which the scheme is based.

2.8 Offshore funds

Offshore funds are not subject to FSA regulation. They are usually based in tax havens such as the Channel Islands or Luxembourg. They may only be marketed to individual UK investors if they are:

- UCITS
- Based in a designated territory
- Individually recognised by the FSA

Designated territories are defined in the Financial Services and Markets Act 2000 and must offer equivalent investor protection. Guernsey, Jersey, the Isle of Man and Bermuda are all designated territories.

Schemes individually recognised by the FSA may be situated in any country where the FSA considers adequate protection is afforded to investors. Such schemes are commonly based in the Republic of Ireland or Luxembourg.

2.9 UCITS

Learning objective	**Know** the purpose and principal features of UCITS

The acronym **'UCITS'** stands for **Undertakings for Collective Investment in Transferable Securities**. It is a term which derives from European regulation, the idea behind it being that once a unit trust qualifies for UCITS status, it is then marketable throughout the **European Economic Area** (EEA). (The EEA comprises the European Union plus Norway, Iceland and Liechtenstein.)

As far as UK unit trusts are concerned, the regulation by the FSA gives a firm background for authorisation as UCITS. This is not, however, automatic and application must be made to the FSA to achieve UCITS status, after which application there is a two-month waiting period.

The UCITS III (Product) Directive was introduced in 2002 to extend the investment and borrowing powers of UCITS recognised schemes. Under UCITS III, investment in derivatives, money market assets and other collective investment schemes (i.e. fund of funds) is now permitted.

2.9.1 Main characteristics of a UCITS fund

- They comply with the provision of the UCITS III (Product) Directive of 2002

- UK schemes must comply with FSA Handbook rules on investment and borrowing powers

- They are funds that invest in securities, derivatives, money market assets and other collective investment schemes

- They are of the open-ended type and allow free redemption of units by investors

- Their units can be freely marketed throughout the EEA, as mentioned above

3 OPEN-ENDED INVESTMENT COMPANIES (OEICs)

Know the definition and legal structure of an OEIC
Know the roles of the Authorised Corporate Director and the Depositary
Know the terms: ICVC, SICAV and the context in which they are used
Know how OEIC shares are priced
Know the ways in which charges can be made by the fund manager
Know how shares are bought and sold
Know how collectives are settled

3.1 OEICs and trading of OEIC shares

Open-Ended Investment Companies (OEICs) are another type of collective investment vehicle which combine some of the features of unit and investment trusts. An OEIC is really a hybrid of these two structures, as it is open-ended like a unit trust, but from a structural perspective is a company and has shares like an investment trust.

Note the different types of **authorised fund** (**unit trust** or **OEIC**), which we outlined in the previous Section of this Chapter.

OEICs are sometimes known by the alternative name '**Investment Company with Variable Capital**' or ICVCs. This is a special company structure, which has been introduced in order to allow a company to continually issue, and redeem, its own shares, and hence their capital structure will vary over time. The end result should be an investment product which is more flexible and more appealing, in particular to the Continental European market.

The shareholders of the OEIC are entitled to vote and to attend shareholder meetings.

A recent development by the London Stock Exchange has been the development of its **extraMARK** market, which allows certain OEIC shares to be traded on SETS. These OEIC shares are known as **Exchange-Traded Funds (ETFs)**, and are discussed later in this Chapter.

Another form of OEIC is an umbrella fund, which allows investors to switch between various sub-funds within one OEIC. OEICs are thus a very flexible form of investment, since sub-funds can be added to an OEIC very quickly, which is another attraction of this structure.

3.2 Operation, pricing and settlement of OEICs

An OEIC must have a board to govern its affairs, one member of which must accept the responsibility of **Authorised Corporate Director** (ACD). The ACD's responsibilities include managing the company's investments, buying and selling its own shares on demand and ensuring the accurate **pricing of shares at net asset value**. This role is thus similar to that of the unit trust manager.

A charge, known as a **dilution levy**, may be made at the discretion of the ACD. The **dilution levy** may be added to the single price, or deducted from the redemption price. The purpose of such a levy is to protect the interests of the shareholders in general and may be charged if the fund is in decline or is experiencing **exceptionally high levels of net sales or redemptions** relative to its size. This levy, if charged, is paid into the fund and not to the managers.

When the investor wishes to **sell** the **OEIC**, the **ACD** will **buy** it. The money value on sale will be based on the **single price** less a **deduction** for **dealing charges**. The price may be further reduced by any **dilution levy**.

The **ACD** may choose to **run a box**. Shares sold back to the ACD will be **kept** and **reissued** to investors, reducing the need for creation and cancellation of shares.

The **register of shareholders** must be **updated daily** and include all shareholdings of the ACD and those held in the box (if there is one) as well as those of the investors.

The role of safeguarding the assets in an OEIC is performed by a **Depositary**.

3.3 OEIC regulation and charges

OEICs are regulated by the FSA, from whom they will require authorisation in a similar way, and following similar rules, to unit trusts. The most significant difference, however, is the requirement for **single pricing**, i.e. the ACD must give one single price at which investors both buy and sell the shares in the OEIC.

The **charge structure** for OEICs is in part determined by OEICs being single priced instruments. Therefore, there is no bid/offer spread. The buying price of the shares in the OEIC reflects the value of the underlying shares, together with any **initial charge**, which will reflect dealing costs and management expenses.

As with **unit trusts** (see earlier), OEICs generally levy **annual management charges**.

3.4 ICVCs and SICAVs

'Investment Companies with Variable Capital (ICVC)' is a term that is interchangeable with 'OEIC'. In the UK we are more likely to use the phrase OEIC, but ICVC is better understood in continental Europe because this is the UK version of a SICAV.

Société d'investissement à capital variables (SICAVs) were originally created in Luxembourg but are now common in Western Europe. As we have seen, they combine many of the features of unit trusts and investment trust companies.

3.5 Fund supermarkets and platforms

A **fund supermarket** or **'platform'**, in the context of the retail financial services sector, is typically an internet-based service for investing in collective investment funds. The 'supermarket' term reflects the way in which they operate; a variety of funds can be purchased from a number of different management groups in one online place. Similar to real life supermarkets, the online counterparts have different goods on offer and services, size and cost vary greatly.

Fund supermarkets, pioneered in the USA, were introduced to the UK investor at the end of 1999. Since their appearance in the market, the choice has become almost overwhelming. In some cases, the UK may be a springboard for fund supermarkets to launch into Europe.

4 INVESTMENT TRUSTS

Know the characteristics of an investment trust: share classes and gearing
Understand the factors that affect the price of an investment trust
Know the meaning of the discounts and premiums in relation to investment trusts
Know how investment trust shares are traded

4.1 The nature of an investment trust company

As with a unit trust, an investment trust (IT) is a collective investment vehicle allowing investors to pool their money. However, unlike unit trusts, OEICs and Exchange-Traded Funds (ETFs – discussed later), ITs are **closed-ended** schemes – there are a limited number of shares for sale. The reason for this is that rather than being a legal trust, an IT is actually a public limited company (plc) with shares listed and traded on the LSE. The purpose of an IT is to invest (mainly) in the securities of other companies.

The investor who wishes to purchase a stake in this collective investment vehicle must buy a share in the company. At any given point there are a limited number of shares in existence, hence the term closed-ended. Should fund managers wish to raise more money they can issue more shares, but this may, of course, take time.

The corporate structure of an UT, however, gives it a further advantage over unit trusts and OEICs because it can freely raise money through borrowing more help it to achieve its objectives. Unit trusts' and OEICs' powers to borrow are substantially more limited. The ability to **borrow** allows an IT to 'gear up' returns for the investor. However, this **gearing** increases the volatility of returns.

4.2 The market in investment trusts

Unlike unit trusts, there is a full secondary market operating in IT shares. They are, after all, shares that trade on the LSE in the same way that the shares of any other company would trade. Pricing is set by **supply and demand** and this will often represent a **discount** to the underlying value of the assets (investments) held by the company. This is different to unit trusts and OEICs, where prices are set according to NAV.

A net asset value can be calculated by looking at the value of each of the underlying shares in the IT and its relative weighting in the fund.

In a simplified example, suppose that an IT comprises the following securities.

Security	Weighting	Net Asset Value (Price × Weighting)
Company A shares worth £5	10% of fund	50p
Company B shares worth £8	20% of fund	160p
Company C shares worth £1	25% of fund	25p
Company D shares worth £2	25% of fund	50p
Company E shares worth £10	20% of fund	200p
	Net Asset Value	485p

If the market price of the share is 436.50p, we would describe this as a 10% discount to net asset value (485p − 436.50p = 48.50p = 10% of 485p).

The level of the discount or premium (a premium being where the share price is higher than the NAV) can vary in line with the following factors.

- The market's view of the quality of the management of the IT. With a highly regarded fund manager the shares of the IT may trade at a price above net asset value, i.e. at a **premium** to NAV. A premium could be a reflection of positive market sentiment towards the fund and the manager's expertise. If a star fund manager leaves, the value of the shares will probably fall.

- Fluctuations in overall stock market levels, for example, giving a bigger discount if the stock market falls, as it is not possible for the IT to re-weight its assets immediately.

4.3 Gearing

Gearing is a measure of the extent of borrowing by an IT and can be calculated as:

$$\frac{\text{Borrowings}}{\text{Capital and reserves}} \times 100$$

For example, if an IT has £100 million of total assets and £14 million of borrowings, shareholders' funds (capital and reserves) are £86 million and gearing is 16.2% (14/86). Gearing, however, increase the volatility of returns.

If the trust's total assets increase or fall by 10% to £110 million or £90 million respectively, and borrowings remain the same at £14 million, the shareholders' funds will have grown to £96 million or fallen to £76 million. This represents an increase or decrease in shareholders' funds of 11.6%, which in both cases is 16% more than the 10% increase or decrease in total assets.

We can say that the shareholders' funds are 16% geared ((14/86) × 100%), or we can express this as a **gearing ratio** of 116 (=(100/86) × 100%).

The **gearing ratio** is expressed as a ratio of total assets to shareholders' funds multiplied by 100.

A gearing ratio of 100 means that there is no gearing. Generally, the higher the gearing factor, the more sensitive an IT's shares will be to the movements up and down in the value of the investment portfolio.

4.4 Split capital investment trusts

4.4.1 Overview

A **split capital investment trust** is like other ITs in that it has a single portfolio of investments. A split capital trust however involves a number of different classes of share, with holders of the different classes having different entitlements to returns of capital or income from the trust.

A split capital trust has a limited life. The period of time remaining to the planned winding up of the trust is usually very significant in how the prices of the different classes of share move.

Split capital investment trusts allow trust managers to tailor returns to appeal to different groups of investors with different strategies, circumstances and attitudes.

The **capital value** of all classes of share will vary up until the trust is wound up. At that stage, the amount of capital returned will depend on the class of share and the order of priority in which the trust is wound up.

5 EXCHANGE-TRADED FUNDS

Exchange-Traded Funds (ETFs) are open-ended collective investment vehicles that are UCITS-compliant and that allow exposure, typically to an **index,** through the purchase of a share at relatively low cost to the investor. They trade and settle like shares, as they are traded through the order book (SETS) and settle through Euroclear UK & Ireland (CREST). The share price, which is quoted throughout the trading day, reflects the value of the investments in the fund.

ETFs must be listed, and are listed on the extraMark market of the LSE. They are eligible for ISA inclusion, and no Stamp Duty Reserve Tax (SDRT) is payable on the purchase of these dematerialised securities, however the investor will pay brokers' commission.

6 HEDGE FUNDS

6.1 Introduction

Hedge funds originally intended to offer investments against the market using derivatives and short selling. Hedge funds have moved away from this and now different hedge funds will have different strategies. Some are geared whilst some consider the macroeconomy and gamble on interest rates and currencies. The one thing that all hedge funds have in common is their desire to search for **absolute returns**.

The hedge fund manager is not concerned about performance compared to benchmarks and therefore has the freedom to try and generate high returns and hence high personal rewards. This will create the need for a risky portfolio, and therefore the name hedge fund is slightly misleading. A better name would probably be isolation fund, since the hedge fund manager looks for specific bets to try and generate high returns.

6.2 Regulation

Hedge funds are not themselves regulated by the FSA and so are not generally marketable investments. However, the fund managers are FSA-regulated firms.

6.3 Types of hedge funds

Hedge funds cover a variety of different investment strategies, including the following.

- **Long/short funds** take positions in stock and are often geared. They are not normally market neutral, but instead have a long or short bias.

- **Market-neutral funds** take long positions in stocks that are considered undervalued and short positions in stocks that are considered overvalued. The fund is sterling neutral, in that the value of short positions is equal to the value of long positions and the sensitivity of long and short positions is the same. Other strategies of a market neutral portfolio are to look for arbitrage opportunities in warrants or derivatives.

- **Global macrofunds** bet on macroeconomic variables such as currencies or interest rates. They are often highly geared and use derivatives. Subgroups of macrofunds are **futures funds**, which use futures to bet on certain asset classes such as currency, fixed income and commodities and **emerging market funds**. These can sometimes be referred to as speculative or tactical funds.

- **Event-driven funds** bet on events specific to a company or security. One example of this would be to invest in distressed securities or shares involved in a merger or acquisition.

Hedge funds typically seek to eliminate or reduce market risk. They are structured as unregulated funds, and require minimum investment levels. They have a great flexibility in the assets they invest in. Finally, hedge funds can borrow money and use derivatives to enhance returns (i.e. 'gear up').

7 REAL ESTATE INVESTMENT TRUSTS (REITs)

Learning objective	**Know** the basic characteristics of REITs: tax efficient; property diversification; liquidity; risk

7.1 Introduction

Real Estate Investment Trusts (REITs) are intended to make it easier to access property as an asset class for a wider range of investors by creating a more liquid and tax-efficient vehicle. A REIT is a company that owns and operates income-producing real estate. Most of the income is distributed to the shareholders and the REIT is exempt from corporation tax. Investors benefit by gaining exposure to property investment and may benefit from diversification since REITs have a low correlation to equities and bonds.

7.2 Key features

A UK-based REIT must meet certain conditions.

- Company must be UK resident, closed-ended and listed on a recognised investment exchange

- No one person can hold more than 10% of the shares

- The tax-exempt property letting part of the business must be ring-fenced from the other activities and should comprise at least 75% of the overall company

- A minimum of 90% of the REIT's net profits from letting must be distributed to investors

- The REIT must withhold basic rate tax on profits distributed to investors

CHAPTER ROUNDUP

- Pooling investments into collective schemes offers diversification to the small investor.

- Collective investments include unit trusts, OEICs, investment trusts ETFs and REITs.

- Unit trusts are open-ended: if more investors wish to buy into the trust, new units are created.

- Units in a unit trust are priced in line with the daily prices of underlying investments. There is typically a spread between bid and offer prices, and the manager also makes money from the annual management charges.

- Open Ended Investment Companies (OEICs) are alternatively called Investment Companies with Variable Capital (ICVCs).

- An OEIC is open-ended, like a unit trust, with pricing in line with underlying asset values. An OEIC is a company, with shares, like an investment trust.

- An investment trust is a Stock Exchange-listed company whose business is to make investments.

- An investment trust is closed-ended, meaning that the number shares is limited. When an investor wants to buy the shares, he or she buys from another investor who already holds the shares.

- The price of shares in the investment trust is established by supply and demand for the shares, which can result in either a discount or premium relative to the value of the underlying assets.

- Exchange-Traded Funds (ETFs) are vehicles comprising baskets of shares reflecting particular indices which these funds are designed to track.

- Unlike with unit trusts and OEICs, the prices of ETFs are adjusted in real time for trading throughout the day.

- Hedge funds are often directed at high net-worth individuals. They are not FSA-regulated and are not generally marketed to the public.

- Traditionally, Hedge funds have used derivatives and short selling (which profits from falls in price of assets). Nowadays, various trading strategies are used by such funds.

- REITs are listed companies that specifically invest in income-producing property.

TEST YOUR KNOWLEDGE

Check your knowledge of the Chapter here, without referring back to the text.

1. Outline the respective roles of the unit trust manager and the trustee.

2. What is the general name given to funds that invest in cash or near-cash instruments?

3. What is indicated by an 'E' against a fund's name in the *Financial Times*?

4. Which types of collective investment are 'open-ended'?

    A   Unit trusts and investment trusts
    B   Investment trust and OEICs
    C   Unit trusts and OEICs
    D   Unit trusts, OEICs and investment trusts

5. Outline the respective roles of the Authorised Corporate Director and the Depositary of an Open Ended Investment Company.

6. The price of shares in an investment trust are a determined primarily by:

    A   Supply and demand for the shares in the market
    B   An FSA formula, reflecting the Net Asset Value
    C   The discount specified by the investment trust company
    D   The ability of the fund manager to create or cancel shares

7. Which one of the following is *not* correct in respect of Exchange Traded Funds (ETFs)?

    A   The funds are listed on the Stock Exchange
    B   ETFs may be included in an Individual Savings Account
    C   Prices are determined daily, by reference to the previous day's valuation
    D   No Stamp Duty Reserve Tax is payable on purchases

8. Which one of the following characteristics are not generally associated with hedge funds?

    A   Emphasis on absolute returns
    B   Long-short strategies
    C   Charging of performance-based fees
    D   FSA regulated

TEST YOUR KNOWLEDGE: ANSWERS

1. The fund manager runs the fund and makes the day-to-day investment management decisions, and appoints the trustee. The job of the trustee is to protect the investor's interests by ensuring that the manager adheres to the rules and regulations that are stipulated in the trust deed. The manager and the trustee are independent of each other.

    See Section 2.1

2. Money market funds.

    See Section 2.3.2

3. That an exit charge may be payable.

    See Section 2.4

4. C is the correct answer. When investors buy unit trusts or OEIC shares, new units are created.

    See Section 3.1

5. The ACD's responsibilities include managing the company's investments, buying and selling its own shares on demand and ensuring the accurate pricing of shares at net asset value. The Depositary's role is to safeguard the assets of the OEIC.

    See Section 3.2

6. A is the correct option. Investment trust shares are listed on the Stock Exchange, and freely traded.

    See Section 4.2

7. C. As with other Stock Exchange listed shares, prices are determined in real time, second-by-second, through the trading day.

    See Section 5

8. D is the correct answer. Hedge funds are not regulated by the FSA.

    See Section 6.2

6

Investment Wrappers

An 'investment wrapper' holds investments within a framework with special rules or tax privileges.

Individual Savings Accounts (ISAs), which are now a familiar part of the UK investment landscape, were introduced in 1999.

More recently introduced are Child Trust Funds (CTFs), the second type of wrapper we consider in this chapter.

CHAPTER CONTENTS

	Page
1 Individual Savings Accounts (ISAs)	111
2 Child Trust Funds	112
Chapter Roundup	114
Test Your Knowledge	115

BPP
LEARNING MEDIA

CHAPTER LEARNING OBJECTIVES

Individual Savings Accounts (ISAs)

- **Know** the definition of and aim of ISAs

- **Know** the tax incentives provided by ISAs

- **Know** the types of ISA available

- **Know** the eligibility conditions for investors

- **Know** the following aspects of investing in ISAs:
    - Subscriptions
    - Transfers
    - Withdrawals
    - Number of managers
    - Number of accounts

Child Trust Funds

- **Know** the tax benefits to a child on the maturity of a child trust fund

- **Know** the main characteristics of child trust funds

1 INDIVIDUAL SAVINGS ACCOUNTS (ISAs)

Know the tax incentives provided by ISAs
Know the definition of and aim of ISAs
Know the types of ISA available
Know the eligibility conditions for investors
Know the following aspects of investing in ISAs: subscriptions; transfers; withdrawals; number of managers; number of accounts

1.1 Introduction

An ISA is an **Individual Savings Account**. The ISA is a form of tax-advantaged savings plan that was introduced in 1999.

ISAs replaced Personal Equity Plans (PEPs), and all existing PEPs have now been converted to ISAs.

In order to be eligible for an ISA, the plan holder must be aged 18 or over and resident in the United Kingdom for tax purposes, except for a cash ISA, which is open to investors aged 16 or over.

It is not possible to hold an ISA jointly or as a trustee for someone else. There is no need to declare ISA income or capital gains on a tax return to HMRC, as **income** and **capital gains** within ISAs are **tax-free**.

1.2 Subscriptions and withdrawals

Subscription limits apply to the total **payments in** to an ISA during the tax year.

The ISA rules allow **withdrawals** at any time without affecting the tax reliefs.

The table below shows the **ISA subscription limits for 2010/11**. (These are the same limits as applied to those aged over 50 from 6 October 2009 – i.e. for 2009/10 – and which apply to all ISA investors from 6 April 2010.)

Overall Maximum	Cash Deposits	Shares, Bonds and Units
£10,200	£5,100	£10,200

- As the table indicates, the subscription limits for the different ISA components have a degree of flexibility. If you do not put the maximum amount into the **cash component**, you can put the excess into the **stocks and shares component**. Thus, during the tax year 2010/11, an individual can invest £10,200 in stocks and shares if he or she has not invested anything in cash deposits.

- **Stocks and shares component**: this component can include shares and corporate bonds issued by companies listed on any recognised stock exchange globally. Almost all OEICs, FSA recognised UCITS funds and UK listed investment trusts (except property investment trusts) and unit trusts will be eligible for inclusion in an ISA. The stocks and shares component can hold eligible **life insurance products** and **medium-term stakeholder products**.

- **Cash component**: this includes bank and building society deposits, units in authorised unit trust money market funds ('cash funds') and 'funds of funds' unit trusts investing in money market funds and **stakeholder products** passing the '5% test', i.e. guaranteeing a return of at least 95% of the capital invested. There is also a National Savings & Investments (NS&I) product which has been designated as a cash ISA.

For subscriptions in a particular tax year, an investor may have one (but only one) manager for a cash ISA and another manager for a stocks and shares ISA, or he may have the same manager for both. If the investor has two managers, it is his responsibility to make sure that his contributions do not exceed the annual limits.

1.3 Transfers

ISA savers are able to **transfer** money saved in a **cash ISA** to their **stocks and shares ISA** without this counting as a new subscription, as follows.

- **The investor can** transfer part or all of their cash ISAs from previous tax years into stocks and shares ISAs, with their present or another provider, without affecting their current annual ISA investment allowance

- **The investor can** transfer money saved in a current tax year cash ISA into a stocks and shares ISA, with their present or another provider. Such a transfer must be for the whole amount saved in that tax year up to the day of the transfer.

ISA managers (who must have HMRC approval) are required to allow **transfers between managers**, although a manager is not required to accept a transfer in.

- The investor may transfer an ISA to a different manager in the year of subscription, in which case the entire ISA subscription for that year must be transferred. After the first year, partial (or full) transfers between ISA managers are permitted.

- Securities within the ISA can be re-registered in the new manager's name. They do not have to be sold and re-purchased.

- If a manager returns ISA proceeds to the investor, this will be treated as a **withdrawal**.

2   CHILD TRUST FUNDS

Learning objectives   **Know** the tax benefits to a child on the maturity of a child trust fund.
Know the main characteristics of child trust funds.

A **child trust fund** (CTF) represents an incentive for family and friends to save for the education of children when they reach university age.

Each child born on or after 1 September 2002 receives a £250 voucher (£500 for low-income families within the child Tax Credit threshold), which the parents can invest into a range of different products from deposit accounts to collective funds and equities.

All **income** and **capital gains tax** are **free of tax** and do not count towards the parents' income. Family and friends may top up the savings to a cumulative total of £1,200 p.a. The Government makes a further £250 contribution when the child reaches age 7 with children in lower income families receiving an additional £250.

The child takes control of the fund at the age of 18 and may spend it as they wish. At age 16, the child can make active decisions on how the money is managed.

Features of CTFs

- A long-term savings and investment account

- Charges capped at 1.5% p.a., and no transfer penalties allowed

- No tax upon income or capital gains

- £250 voucher to start each child's account

- Maximum of £1,200 each year can be added, with minimum subscription set no higher than £10

- Child has access to the fund at the age of 18

- Although the fund is free of tax up to the age of 18, on maturity it would revert to an ordinary fund subjected to tax

- When the child reaches the age of 13, a percentage (20%) of the money invested in securities can be moved into cash each year so that by the age of 18 all the fund is held as cash

CHAPTER ROUNDUP

- ISAs offer a tax-incentivised wrapper for holding cash and shares, within the specified investment limits.

- An overall subscription limit applies for an individual's ISA subscriptions in the tax year. The whole of this limit can be invested in a stocks and shares ISA if desired. A lower sub-limit applies to the amount invested in a cash ISA.

- ISAs can be transferred between managers, and money in cash ISAs can be transferred to a stocks and shares ISA.

- The Government will make a starting contribution to a Child Trust Fund for children born since 1 September 2002, and family members may top up these contributions. Income and capital gains are free of tax, and the funds are available to the child at age 18.

TEST YOUR KNOWLEDGE

Check your knowledge of the Chapter here, without referring back to the text.

1.   What is the minimum age at which someone can open a cash ISA?

2.   Which one of the following is a feature of ISAs?

  A No capital gains tax
  B Income tax relief on contributions
  C Reclaim of tax credits on dividends
  D Can be held jointly with a spouse

3.   Michelle, aged 56, holds an ISA and has, so far in the current tax year 2010/11, invested £2,000 which has been used to buy company shares within the ISA. How much more can she invest in 2010/11 in stocks and shares within the ISA?

4.   The annual management charge for a Child Trust Fund is capped at

  A 0.25%
  B 0.5%
  C 1.0%
  D 1.5%

TEST YOUR KNOWLEDGE: ANSWERS

1.   16 years.

     See Section 1.1

2.   A is the correct answer. There is no CGT to pay on ISAs.

     See Section 1.1

3.   £10,200 – £2,000 = **£8,200**.

     See Section 1.2

4.   Charges are capped at 1.5% p.a.

     See Section 2

7

Financial Services Regulation

The role of the Financial Service Authority, as a regulator with strong statutory powers, is central to the operation of financial services businesses in the UK.

Knowledge of the rules designed to prevent money laundering is important for all working in the industry. There is legislation and regulation designed to prevent abuse of markets, including insider dealing.

The regulation of UK financial services is also affected by international events and in this chapter we look at the role played by the European Commission and the Committee of European Securities Regulators.

Data protection legislation imposes requirements on financial services businesses, as for all other types of business.

What procedures must be followed if a customer has a complaint? We examine the regulations, and also the compensation arrangements that come into play if a financial service business fails.

CHAPTER CONTENTS

		Page
1	The Development of Financial Services Regulation	119
2	Financial Services and Markets Act (FSMA) 2000	121
3	Financial Crime	125
4	Insider Dealing and Market Abuse	129
5	Data Protection Act 1998	131
6	Breaches, Complaints and Compensation	132
	Chapter Roundup	137
	Test Your Knowledge	139

CHAPTER LEARNING OBJECTIVES

Financial Services and Markets Act

- **Know** the function of the following in the financial services industry: Regulators (FSA, EC Commission, Committee of European Securities Regulators)

- **Understand** the need for regulation and the purpose of the Financial Services and Markets Act 2000

- **Know** the four statutory objectives of the Financial Services Authority

- **Understand** the reasons for authorisation of firms and approved persons

- **Know** the purpose of the FSA's principles-based approach to regulation

- **Know** the five groups of activities (controlled functions) requiring approved person status

- **Know** the FSA's six outcomes for treating customers fairly

- **Know** the role of the Financial Services and Markets Tribunal

Financial Crime

- **Know** what money laundering is and the related criminal offences

- **Know** the purpose and main provisions of the Proceeds of Crime Act 2002 and the Money Laundering Regulations 2007

- **Understand** the three main stages of money laundering

- **Know** the action to be taken by those employed in financial services if money laundering activity is suspected

- **Know** what constitutes satisfactory evidence of identity

Insider Dealing and Market Abuse

- **Know** the offences that constitute insider dealing and the instruments covered

- **Know** the offences that constitute market abuse and the instruments covered

Data Protection Act 1998

- **Understand** the impact of the Data Protection Act 1998 on firms' activities

Breaches, Complaints and Compensation

- **Know** the difference between a breach and a complaint

- **Know** the responsibilities of the industry for handling customer complaints and dealing with breaches

- **Know** the role of the Financial Ombudsman Service

- **Know** the circumstances under which the Financial Services Compensation Scheme pays compensation and the compensation payable for investment claims

1   THE DEVELOPMENT OF FINANCIAL SERVICES REGULATION

Know the function of the following in the financial services industry: Regulators (FSA, EC Commission, Committee of European Securities Regulators)
Understand the need for regulation and the purpose of the Financial Services and Markets Act 2000

1.1 Development of the UK regulatory system

1.1.1 Creation of a single regulator

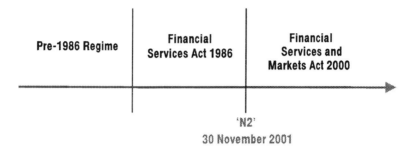

'N2'
30 November 2001

Before the advent of the **Financial Services Act 1986**, the UK financial services industry was entirely self-regulating. Standards were maintained by an assurance that those in the financial services industry had a common set of values and were able, and willing, to ostracise those who violated them.

The 1986 Act moved the UK to a system which became known as '**self-regulation within a statutory framework**'. Once **authorised**, firms and individuals would be regulated by self-regulating organisations (SROs), such as IMRO, SFA or PIA. The Financial Services Act 1986 only covered investment activities. Retail banking, general insurance, Lloyd's of London and mortgages were all covered by separate Acts and Codes.

When the Labour Party gained power in 1997, it wanted to make change to the regulation of financial services. The late 1990s saw a more radical reform of the financial services system with the unification of most aspects of financial services regulation under a **single statutory regulator**, the **Financial Services Authority (FSA)**. The process took place in two phases.

1.1.2 Phases of the reforms

First, the Bank of England's responsibility for banking supervision was transferred to the **Financial Services Authority (FSA)** as part of the **Bank of England Act 1998**. Despite losing responsibility for banking supervision, the **Bank of England** ('the Bank') gained the role in 1998 of **setting official UK interest rates**.

The Bank is also responsible for maintaining stability in the financial system by analysing and promoting initiatives to strengthen the financial system. It is also the financial system's '**lender of last resort**', being ready to provide funds in exceptional circumstances.

The **second phase** of reforms consisted of a new Act covering financial services which would repeal the main provisions of the Financial Services Act 1986 and some other legislation. The earlier 'patchwork quilt' of regulation would be swept away and the FSA would regulate investment business, insurance business, banking, building societies, Friendly Societies, mortgages and Lloyd's.

On 30 November 2001, the new Act – the **Financial Services and Markets Act 2000 (FSMA 2000)** – came into force, to create a system of **statutory regulation**. While practitioners and consumers are actively consulted, it is the FSA that co-ordinates the regulation of the industry.

The new regime seeks to learn from many of the regulatory failures that occurred during the 1980s and 1990s. Undoubtedly, the most important has been that of pensions mis-selling, where salesmen encouraged some 2.2 million people to move out of their employers' schemes into personal pension plans. These transfers were often unsuitable and have given rise to some major compensation claims. This has led to an increased importance in the new regime on educating investors to ensure that they understand the risks of transactions.

1.2 FSA as the UK statutory regulator

The creation of the FSA as the UK's **single statutory regulator** for the industry brought together regulation of investment, insurance and banking.

With the implementation of FSMA 2000 at date 'N2' in 2001, the FSA took over responsibility for:

- **Prudential supervision** of all firms, which involves monitoring the adequacy of their management, financial resources and internal systems and controls, and

- **'Conduct of business' regulations** of those firms engaged in investment business. This involves overseeing firms' dealings with investors to ensure, for example, that information provided is clear and not misleading

Arguably, the FSA's role as **legislator** has been diminished by the requirements of EU Single Market Directives – in particular, the far-reaching **Markets in Financial Instruments Directive (MiFID)**, implemented on 1 November 2007 – as the FSA has increasingly needed to apply rules which have been formulated at the **European level**.

1.3 Other regulators

1.3.1 The European Commission

The **European Commission** is a politically independent institution that aims to uphold the interests of the EU as a whole. Member states appoint Commissioners to sit on the Commission. These are often former politicians. The Commissioners meet on a weekly basis and are supported by a huge number of civil servants.

The Commission proposes legislation to the Council and Parliament, and manages and implements EU policy. The Commission also enforces EU law together with the European Court of Justice and represents the EU internationally.

Such legislation includes the Market Abuse Directive (MAD), the Capital Requirements Directive (CRD) and the Markets in Financial Instruments Directive (MiFID).

1.3.2 The Committee of European Securities Regulators (CESR)

The so-called 'Committee of Wise Men, chaired by Baron Alexandre Lamfalussy, outlined in its report of February 2001 several shortcomings in the legislative system for securities. The committee also proposed the creation of an independent committee of European securities regulators, which is called the **Committee of European Securities Regulators** and was established in 2001.

CESR make-up

- Each EU member state has one member.

- The members – nominated by the member states – are heads of the national public authorities competent in the field of securities.

- The European Commission is represented by its Director General.

CESR role

- To improve coordination among securities regulators
- To act as an advisory group assisting the European Commission
- To work on the implementation of community legislation in EU member states

2 FINANCIAL SERVICES AND MARKETS ACT (FSMA) 2000

Understand the need for regulation and the purpose of the Financial Services and Markets Act 2000
Know the four statutory objectives of the Financial Services Authority
Understand the reasons for authorisation of firms and approved persons
Know the purpose of the FSA's principles-based approach to regulation
Know the five groups of activities (controlled functions) requiring approved person status
Know the FSA's six outcomes for treating customers fairly
Know the role of the Financial Services and Markets Tribunal

2.1 Regulatory structure

FSMA 2000 provides the framework of the regulatory system, with much of the detail being provided by secondary legislation. The secondary legislation links into various sections of FSMA, fleshing out the requirements and thus requiring the two to be read in conjunction. An example of this is with regard to the authorisation requirement. FSMA 2000 requires that any firm undertaking a **regulated activity** must be **authorised** or exempt (the authorisation or exemption is primarily obtained through direct approach to the FSA). Whilst ways that a firm may obtain authorisation are contained in FSMA, the specific definition of what is a 'regulated activity' and the exemptions are found in secondary legislation – namely the Regulated Activities Order 2001. Both FSMA 2000 and the secondary legislation were drafted by **HM Treasury**.

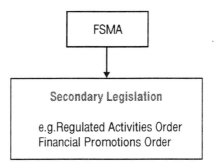

2.2 FSA's statutory objectives

Section 2 of FSMA 2000 spells out the purpose of regulation by specifying **four statutory objectives**. The emphasis placed on these objectives makes FSMA unusual compared to the Acts that it supersedes, none of which clearly articulated their objectives. FSMA seeks to inject clarity into what the regulatory regime is trying to achieve and, perhaps more importantly, seeks to manage expectations regarding what it cannot achieve.

It is the responsibility of the FSA to carry out the statutory objectives summarised below.

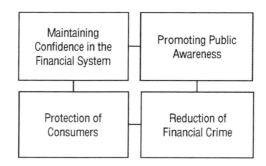

- **Market confidence**. The regulator seeks to ensure the absence of market manipulation and, more broadly, to ensure that the public can trust the soundness of the banking and financial system.

- **Public awareness**. An innovative feature of the objectives is to try to raise levels of financial literacy among the general public. This springs from a recognition that people need information and understanding if they are to make responsible choices about investments and savings.

- **Protection of consumers**. Investor protection is a fundamental aim, but the system recognises that there are several different types of consumers and seeks to deliver the appropriate levels of protection.

- **Reduction of financial crime**. The final objective seeks to reduce financial crime – from money laundering to insider dealing. Note that although eliminating financial crime completely would be ideal, it is recognised that this might be an unrealistic objective.

2.3 Authorisation

Following on from the statutory objectives of FSMA 2000 are a number of **principles of good regulation**, including the ideal that only certain firms, meeting FSA-stipulated criteria, may be allowed to carry out **regulated activities**.

S19 FSMA 2000 is known as the **General Prohibition**, which states that no person (the definition of person includes both companies and individuals) may carry out regulated activities in the UK unless they are **authorised** (licensed) to do so or are **exempt** from the requirement to seek authorisation.

Authorisation is commonly obtained from the FSA according to Part IV of FSMA 2000 and hence is often referred to as **'Part IV Permission'**. Firms are sent an application pack which requires detailed information regarding the applicant's business. The applicant is also required to pay a fee. The FSA then has six months to determine an authorisation from the date of receipt. The FSA must be satisfied that a firm seeking permission is **'fit and proper'** and that it meets, and continues to satisfy, the **threshold conditions** for the activity concerned.

These threshold conditions relate to:

- **Legal status**, i.e. legal structure of the business

- **Location of offices**, i.e. within the UK if the applicant is a UK company

- The effect of **close links** of the applicant with other entities

- **Adequate capital and human resources**

- The firm being **'fit and proper'**, i.e. competent management and having appropriate procedures in place to comply with regulations

2.4 Approved persons

Just as **firms** require **authorisation** to conduct regulated activities, **individuals** working within specified functions must be **approved** to perform their function. The FSA has published a list of controlled functions, of which a summary of the main categories is provided below.

- **Governing functions**, e.g. directors, partners, the chief executive
- **Required functions,** e.g. compliance officers, money laundering reporting officers
- **Systems and control functions,** e.g. risk assessment, internal audit
- **Significant management functions,** e.g. insurance underwriting, head of settlement
- **Customer functions,** e.g. investment adviser, pension transfer specialist, customer trading

Any person performing one of these controlled functions must obtain approved person status first. Approved persons are then subject to a set of principles or rules set down by the FSA. They agree to follow this particular set of rules and agree to be subject to the FSA's discipline should a breach of these rules occur.

2.5 FSA's approach to regulation

After the establishment of the FSA, there were concerns about the extensive nature of regulation, and the volume of regulatory material which firms were having to follow.

A 'twin approach' was heralded by the FSA, combining 'risk-based' and 'principles-based' aspects.

- The FSA's **risk-based approach** means that it focuses attention on those institutions and activities that are likely to pose the greatest risk to consumers and markets. The FSA considers it both impossible and undesirable to remove all risk from the financial system.

- The '**principles-based**' approach implies that, rather than formulate detailed rules to cover the varied circumstances firms are involved in, the Authority would expect firms to carry more responsibility in making their own judgement about how to apply the regulatory Principles and Statements of Principle to their business. The switch to **more principles-based regulation** means that firms need to develop more of their own internal rules. The emphasis of the regulator is on the **outcomes** achieved rather than on the rules followed, and so the term '**outcomes-based regulation**' is also sometimes used. The FSA's initiative on **Treating Customers Fairly (TCF)** (see below) is an example of the Authority's emphasis on over-arching principles, and on consumer outcomes.

Since the introduction of the 'more principles-based' approach, there has been progress towards reduction in the volume of detailed rules. The incorporation of new **MiFID** rules has helped this process, because the requirements of the MiFID Directive are generally less wordy and less detailed than the previous FSA rules which have been replaced.

The impact of principles-based regulation has also been seen in **enforcement cases**, where the FSA has relied on its expectation that firms would follow higher-level principles, even where there might not have been breaches of detailed rules. The FSA was deliberately shifting responsibility on to firms to decide what higher level principles mean for them.

Exam tip

> Be sure to understand the purpose of principles-based regulation: a 'hot' topic added to the syllabus in 2009.

With the collapse of Northern Rock and financial turmoil in other institutions and in financial markets during 2007 and 2008 particularly, the FSA was criticised for its role in the unfolding events. What had come to be seen as a **'light touch' regulatory regime** was being called into question. The FSA responded with a strengthened supervisory programme, and further reforms may be seen in the future.

2.6 Treating customers fairly (TCF)

In addition to meeting the regulatory objectives, the FSA aims to maintain efficient, orderly and clean markets and help retail customers achieve a fair deal. Since 2000, the FSA has examined what a fair deal for retail customers actually means and this has led to much discussion of the concept of **TCF** – 'treating customers fairly'.

The FSA does not define **treating customers fairly (TCF)** in a way that applies in all circumstances. By adopting a '**principles-based approach**' to TCF through Principle 6, the FSA puts the onus on firms to determine what is fair in each particular set of circumstances. Firms therefore need to make their own assessment of what TCF means for them, taking into account the nature of their business.

The FSA wants firms to focus on delivering the following **six TCF consumer outcomes**.

1. Consumers can be confident that they are dealing with firms where the **fair treatment** of customers is central to the corporate culture.

2. **Products and services** marketed and sold in the retail market are designed to **meet** the **needs** of identified consumer groups and are targeted accordingly.

3. Consumers are provided with **clear information** and are kept appropriately informed before, during and after the point of sale.

4. Where consumers receive advice, the **advice is suitable** and takes account of their circumstances.

5. Consumers are provided with **products** that **perform as firms have led them to expect**, and the associated service is both of an acceptable standard and also as they have been led to expect.

6. **Consumers do not face unreasonable post-sale barriers** imposed by firms to change product, switch provider, submit a claim or make a complaint.

Exam tip

> The six TCF outcomes above form another topic added to the syllabus in 2009.

2.7 The Financial Service and Markets Tribunal

FSMA 2000 makes provision for an independent body accountable to the **Ministry of Justice** (formerly the Department for Constitutional Affairs) which was established under the **Financial Services and Markets Tribunal Rules 2001**.

The **Financial Services and Markets Tribunal (FSMT)** provides for a complete rehearing of FSA enforcement and authorisation cases where the firm or individual and the FSA have not been able to agree the outcome. Therefore, if a firm or individual receives a Decision Notice or Supervisory Notice or is refused authorisation or approval, it may refer this to the Tribunal. The Tribunal will determine what appropriate action the FSA should take and in doing so can consider any new evidence which has come to light since the original decision was made.

3 FINANCIAL CRIME

Know what money laundering is and the related criminal offences
Know the purpose and main provisions of the Proceeds of Crime Act 2002 and the Money Laundering Regulations 2007
Understand the three main stages of money laundering
Know the action to be taken by those employed in financial services if money laundering activity is suspected
Know what constitutes satisfactory evidence of identity

3.1 Money laundering

Money laundering is a process by which money from illegal sources is made to appear to have been legally derived. Through a variety of methods, the nature, source and ownership of such criminal proceeds are concealed. By illegal sources, we mean any type of conduct that would be illegal and criminal in the UK, including tax evasion, drug trafficking or arms dealing.

3.2 Stages of money laundering

Money laundering can be broken down into three typical stages as follows.

- **Placement** – the investment of the proceeds of criminal activity

- **Layering** – the mingling of the money from an illegal source with that from a legitimate source. 'Separation' occurs at this stage

- **Integration** – the withdrawal and usage of the now undetectable proceeds of criminal activity

3.3 Anti-money laundering legislation and regulations

In 1991, the European Union adopted a **Money Laundering Directive** on the prevention of the use of the financial system for the purpose of money laundering. The Directive stipulated certain **internal procedures and controls** for EU financial and credit institutions. It also required EU member states to implement legislation making it a **criminal offence** for individuals to assist in money laundering. Second and third Directives followed in 2001 and 2007 respectively, and the latest UK regulations are the **Money Laundering Regulations 2007**.

Aims of internal procedures and controls

- **Deterrence** – to prevent credit and financial institutions being used for money laundering purposes

- **Co-operation** – to ensure that there is co-operation between credit and financial institutions and law enforcement agencies

- **Detection** – to establish customer identification and record-keeping procedures within all financial and credit institutions to assist the law enforcement agencies in detecting, tracing and prosecuting money launderers

The **Criminal Justice Act 1993 (CJA 1993)** implemented the requirements of the first Money Laundering Directive to make certain activities committed by individuals a criminal offence.

Various provisions of the CJA have been repealed and replaced by provisions in the **Proceeds of Crime Act 2002 (POCA 2002)**. POCA consolidates and updates the money laundering requirements which apply to individuals. Part 7 of POCA makes laundering the proceeds of any criminal activity illegal.

The **Assets Recovery Agency** has been set up to recover illegally gained assets.

3.4 Assistance

3.4.1 Offence

If any person knowingly helps another person to launder the proceeds of drug trafficking or criminal conduct or to launder terrorist funds, he will be committing an offence. The legislation therefore covers laundering of the proceeds of **any serious crime**.

3.4.2 Possible defence

It is a defence to the above offences that a person **disclosed** his knowledge or belief concerning the origins of the property either to the police or to the appropriate officer in his firm.

3.4.3 Penalty

The maximum penalty for any offence of assisting a money launderer is **14 years' imprisonment and/or an unlimited fine**.

3.5 Failure to report

3.5.1 Money laundering reporting officer

All financial institutions must appoint an appropriate person within the organisation, generally known as the **Money Laundering Reporting Officer (MLRO)**.

Functions of the MLRO

- To receive reports of transactions giving rise to knowledge or suspicion of money laundering activities from employees of the institution: **employees** in financial institutions **who suspect** money laundering activity **should report** their concerns to their firm's MLRO.

> **Examples of suspicious activity**
>
> - No discernible need to use the firm
> - Unnecessary use of an intermediary
> - Reluctant verification
> - Unusual trading patterns
> - Introduction from a suspicious jurisdiction
> - Non-market price transactions
> - Use of bearer securities
> - Payments to third parties

- To determine whether a report of a suspicious transaction from the employee, considered together with all other relevant information, does actually give rise to knowledge or suspicion of money laundering

- If, after consideration, the MLRO knows or suspects that money laundering is taking place, to report those suspicions to the **Serious Organised Crime Agency (SOCA)**

For the purpose of each individual employee, it is important to note that a report made to the money laundering reporting officer concerning a transaction means that the employee has fulfilled his statutory obligations and will have **no criminal liability** in relation to any money laundering offence in respect of the reported transaction.

3.5.2 Offence

If a person **within the regulated sector** discovers information during the course of his employment that makes him **know or suspect** money laundering is occurring, he must inform the police or the appropriate officer of the firm as soon as possible. Failure to report the matter as soon as is reasonably practicable is a criminal offence.

3.5.3 Possible defence

The only defence to this charge is if a person charged can prove that he had a **reasonable excuse** for failing to disclose this information. Whether an excuse is reasonable will depend on the circumstances of the case, but it is noteworthy that the person charged has the burden of proving that he had a reasonable excuse for his failure to disclose.

The relevant legislation specifically provides that any person making a disclosure of this kind will not be in breach of any duty of confidentiality owed to a customer.

3.5.4 Penalty

This offence is punishable with a maximum of **five years' imprisonment and/or an unlimited fine**.

3.6 Tipping off

3.6.1 Offence

Even where suspicions are reported, the parties must generally be careful **not to alert the suspicions of the alleged launderer** since, within the regulated sector, this can itself amount to an offence.

A person **within the regulated sector** commits an offence if, based on information they acquire in the course of business that is likely to prejudice any investigation, they **disclose** that an investigation is under way, or that firm's money laundering officer or the authorities have been informed.

There are some exceptions, for example for disclosures made within a financial institution or group, or between professional advisers. Another exception is a disclosure by a professional adviser to their client if it is for the purpose of dissuading the client from committing an offence.

3.6.2 Possible defences

A **defence** against the tipping off offences is that the person does not know or suspect that the disclosure is likely to prejudice an investigation.

Once again, the burden of proving the defence rests upon the person who has been charged with the offence.

3.6.3 Penalty

Tipping off is punishable with a maximum of **two years' imprisonment and/or an unlimited fine.**

3.7 Penalties: Summary

Offence	Maximum penalty: Crown Court	Maximum penalty: Magistrates Court
Assistance	14 years and an unlimited fine	6 months and a £5,000 fine
Failure to report	5 years and an unlimited fine	6 months and a £5,000 fine
Tipping off	2 years and an unlimited fine	3 months and a £5,000 fine

3.8 Evidence of identity

Firms are expected to 'know their customers'. Based on an **assessment of the money laundering / terrorist financing risk** that each customer presents, the firm will need to:

- **Verify the customer's identity (ID)** – determining exactly who the customer is

- **Collect additional 'KYC' (Know Your Customer) information**, and keep such information **current and valid** – to understand the customer's circumstances and business, and (where appropriate) the sources of funds or wealth, or the purpose of specific transactions

Many customers, by their nature or through what is already known about them by the firm, carry a **lower** money laundering or terrorist financing **risk**. These might include:

- Customers who are employment-based or with a regular source of income from a known source
- Customers with a long-term and active business relationship with the firm
- Customers represented by those who are subject to court ratification (such as executors)

The Money Laundering Regulations 2007 specify detailed **customer due diligence (CDD)** procedures, which involve:

- Identifying the customer and verifying his identity

- Identifying the beneficial owner (taking measures to understand the ownership and control structure, in the case of a company or trust) and verifying his identity

- Obtaining information on the purpose and intended nature of the business relationship

A firm must apply CDD when it:

- Establishes a business relationship
- Carries out an occasional transaction, of €15,000 or more
- Suspects money laundering or terrorist financing
- Doubts the veracity of identification or verification documents

How much identity information to ask for in the course of **CDD**, and what to verify, are matters **for the judgement of the firm**, based on its **assessment of risk**.

Documents offering evidence of identity are seen in the JMLSG Guidance Notes as forming the following broad hierarchy according to who has issued them, in the following order:

- Government departments or a court
- Other public sector bodies
- Regulated financial services firms
- Other firms subject to MLR or equivalent legislation
- Other organisations

As well as standard CDD there is:

- **Enhanced due diligence (EDD)** – for higher risk situations, customers not physically present when identities are verified, correspondent banking and **politically exposed persons** (PEPs)

- **Simplified due diligence (SDD)** – which may be applied to certain financial sector firms, companies listed on a regulated market, UK public authorities, child trust funds and certain pension funds and low risk products

EDD procedures when a customer is not present include obtaining additional documents, data or information to those specified below, requiring certification by a financial services firm and ensuring that an initial payment is from a bank account in the customer's name.

The category of **'politically exposed persons' (PEPs)** comprises higher ranking Government officials of foreign governments and Members of Parliaments, except of the UK Parliament, and the immediate families and close associates of such persons. PEPs can pose a **higher risk** because their position may make them vulnerable to corruption. Senior management approval (from an immediate superior) should be sought for establishing a business relationship with such a customer and adequate measures should be taken to establish sources of wealth and of funds.

SDD means not having to apply CDD measures. In practice, this means not having to identify the customer, or to verify the customer's identity, or, where relevant, that of a beneficial owner, nor having to obtain information on the purpose or intended nature of the business relationship.

Failure to implement the measures required by **MLR 2007** is a criminal offence, punishable with a maximum sentence of two years' imprisonment for any senior officer of the firm and/or an unlimited fine, irrespective of whether money laundering has taken place.

4 INSIDER DEALING AND MARKET ABUSE

ing objectives   **Know** the offences that constitute insider dealing and the instruments covered.
Know the offences that constitute market abuse and the instruments covered.

4.1 Insider dealing: definition

Insider dealing is the offence of acting with information that is not freely and openly available to all other participants in the market place. **Part V** of the **Criminal Justice Act 1993** makes it a **criminal offence** for connected persons who receive inside information to act on that information.

4.2 Insider dealing offences

If a person satisfies the definition of an insider, it is an offence to:

- **Deal** in the affected securities either on a regulated market or through a professional intermediary
- **Encourage another** person to deal (e.g. a friend or family member)
- **Disclose the information** to another person other than in the proper performance of their duties

Insider dealing legislation covers shares, debt securities issued by the private or public sector, warrants, depository receipts, options, futures or Contracts for Difference, or any of the above.

An insider is defined as a person who has **information** in his possession which he **knows** is inside information and which he **knows** is from an inside source. Information in this context refers to **unpublished price-sensitive information**, which is specific or precise and relates to a security or its issuer. Consequently, acting on a general market rumour would not be insider dealing.

An insider must be **an individual** (i.e. not a company) and would include a **director, employee** or **shareholder** of an issuer of securities or a person having access to the information by virtue of employment, office or profession. A person will also be an insider if he receives the information either directly or indirectly from one of the above and satisfies the general definition above.

The legislation covers the following instruments.

- Shares
- Debt securities issued by the private or public sector
- Warrants
- Depositary receipts

- Options, futures or Contracts For Difference (CfDs) on any of the above

(A **CfD** is a way of taking a long or short position in an underlying instrument without paying the full value of the instrument. The CfD thus offers geared exposure to price changes in the underlying instrument.)

4.3 Market abuse

Market abuse is an offence introduced by S118 of FSMA to provide an alternative regime for enforcing the prohibition on insider dealing and misleading statements/practices.

The **territorial scope** of the offence is very wide. It covers everyone, not just authorised firms and approved persons. Furthermore, firms or persons outside the UK are also covered by the offence.

As market abuse is a **civil offence**, the FSA must prove, on the balance of probabilities, that a person:

- Engaged in market abuse; or

- By taking or refraining from action, required or encouraged another person to engage in market abuse.

The Table below gives a high level summary of the market abuse offence. You will see that there are seven types of behaviour that can amount to market abuse.

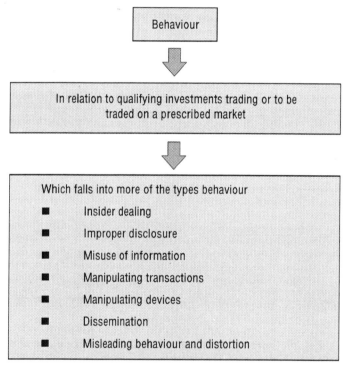

Behaviour can include both action and inaction. Such behaviour must occur in relation to **qualifying investments** traded on a **prescribed market,** i.e. investments traded on a Recognised Investment Exchange (RIE) or other regulated market. It must also be likely to be regarded by a regular user of the market as a failure on the part of the person concerned to observe the standard of behaviour reasonably expected of a person in his position in relation to the market.

The use of the words 'in relation to' means that the behaviour need not occur **on** the prescribed market as long as the behaviour **relates to** an investment which **can be** traded on a prescribed market, e.g. abusive trading of a non-exchange traded Brent Crude Oil futures contract can be market abuse, as Brent Crude Oil futures **can be** traded on a RIE (**ICE Futures**).

5 DATA PROTECTION ACT 1998

Understand the impact of the Data Protection Act 1998 on firms' activities

Under the **Data Protection Act 1998 (DPA 1998)** where persons are processing personal data, whether electronically or manually, they must (unless exempt) be registered with the **Information Commissioner** who maintains a public registry of data controllers and comply with the provisions of the DPA. The requirements apply to most organisations no matter how small and covers all personal data whether it relates to clients, employees, suppliers or any other person.

Under the DPA 1998 there are **eight Data Protection Principles** (sometimes called the principles of good information handling) which those controlling personal data must comply with.

- **Principle 1** – Personal data shall be **processed fairly and lawfully**. This requires that data shall not be processed unless consent has been obtained from the subject of the data, or the processing is necessary to comply with legal obligations or to protect the vital interests of the subject of the data. Protection of vital interests could be where medical details need to be passed as a result of an accident.

  In addition, where the data is 'sensitive personal data' (e.g. regarding ethnic origin, religion, health, or criminal record) additional requirements are imposed to handle such data.

- **Principle 2** – Personal data shall be obtained only for specified and lawful purposes and shall only be processed in a manner that is compatible with those purposes.

- **Principle 3** – Personal data shall be **adequate, relevant and not excessive** in relation to the purpose or purposes for which they are processed. This is to ensure no more data is held on a person than is strictly required in the circumstances.

- **Principle 4** – Personal data shall be **accurate** and, where necessary, kept up to date. This requires reasonable steps to be taken to ensure the accuracy of the data.

- **Principle 5** – Personal data processed for any purpose(s) shall **not be kept for longer** than is necessary for that purpose(s). Data should be reviewed regularly to determine whether it can be deleted.

- **Principle 6** – Personal data shall only be processed in accordance with data subjects, i.e. in accordance with the wishes of those individuals who are the subjects of the data.

- **Principle 7** – Appropriate **technical and organisational measures** shall be taken against unauthorised or unlawful processing of personal data and against accidental loss or destruction of, or damage to, personal data. Consideration should therefore be taken as to those members of staff accessing data and the technology used to store such data.

- **Principle 8** – Personal data shall **not be transferred** to a country or territory outside the EEA, unless that country or territory ensures an adequate level of protection of the rights and freedoms of data subjects in relation to the processing of personal data. Guidance as to which countries comply with these requirements can be obtained from the Information Commissioner.

In essence, to comply with DPA 1998, firms should be open with individuals about information held about them and very careful about passing that information to third parties.

Where breaches occur the Information Commissioner has **wide powers** to issue enforcement notices requiring the data controller to take certain action to remedy any breaches. Breaches of the DPA requirements are punishable by a maximum fine of £5,000 in the Magistrates' Court and unlimited fines in the Crown Court. There are also powers to enter premises and seize documents with a court warrant.

As a result of DPA 1998, authorised firms should be aware that records required to be obtained and kept under FSA rules (e.g. money laundering identification requirements) must also comply with the requirements of DPA 1998.

6 BREACHES, COMPLAINTS AND COMPENSATION

Learning objectives

Know the difference between a breach and a complaint.
Know the responsibilities of the industry for handling customer complaints and dealing with breaches.
Know the role of the Financial Ombudsman Service.
Know the circumstances under which the Compensation Scheme pays compensation and the compensation payable for investment claims.

6.1 Breaches and complaints

A breach occurs when an authorised firm fails to obey the rules of the FSA or any other regulatory legislation, such as FSMA 2000. In this instance the matter should be directed to the FSA and the FSA will investigate and take appropriate action.

A complaint occurs when a client makes direct contact with a firm, verbally or in writing, to express dissatisfaction about how they have been treated.

6.1.1 Customer complaints – Internal procedures

Firms may receive complaints from their clients about the way the firm has provided financial services or in respect of failure to provide a financial service. This could include allegations of financial loss whether or not such losses have actually yet occurred. Under the FSA's rules, a firm must have procedures to ensure complaints **from eligible complainants** are properly handled. A complaint is defined as 'any **oral or written** expression of dissatisfaction for, or on behalf of, an **eligible complainant** whether justified or not'.

Eligible complainants comprise private individuals, businesses with a group annual turnover of less than £1m and charities with an annual income of less than £1m or trusts with net asset value of less than £1m (other than intermediate customers or market counterparties) who are customers or potential customers of the firm.

The firm's procedures need to cover:

- **Receiving complaints**: the proper handling of complaints from customers relevant to its compliance with the regulatory system.

- **Responding to complaints**: strict time limits are set out for this process.

- **Investigation of complaints**: in order that the appropriate remedial action to those complaints is promptly taken.

- Where the complaint is not promptly remedied, that the customer is advised of any further avenues of complaint available, in particular, their right to use the **Financial Ombudsman Service (FOS)**.

A firm must properly **publicise its complaint procedures** by:

- Referring in writing to the availability of the procedures at or immediately after the point of sale, e.g. in a client agreement, terms of business or key features document.

- Supplying copies on request and automatically where a complaint is received (unless the complaint is resolved by the end of the next business day).

- Displaying in all branches a notice indicating it is covered by the FOS.

The procedures must be in **writing** and designed to ensure that:

- Each **employee or appointed representative** dealing with a customer is aware of the procedures.

- The complaint is **investigated promptly and fully** by a senior, uninvolved person with authority to settle the matter (or ready access to someone who has the authority). This person must be specifically named in the copy of procedures given to the customer. Responses must adequately address the subject matter and offer fair redress where appropriate.

- A copy of a written complaint and the firm's response and record of any action taken are **recorded and kept for at least three years** from the date of the receipt of the complaint. This must include the name of the complainant, the substance of the complaint and all correspondence and redress offered by the firm.

The firm must ensure it has **appropriate management controls** to ensure the complaints rules are complied with and that these systems enable management to identify any recurring or systemic problems that are identified.

The FSA sets out **time limits** for firms dealing with complaints where there is an allegation of financial loss (note that complaints can still be made where losses have not yet crystallised, e.g. pensions mis-selling). A firm must send a written acknowledgement and a copy of the complaints procedure within **five** business days of receipt of the complaint, giving the name or job title of the person handling the complaint together with the firm's procedures. However, this does not apply where a complaint has been resolved by close of business on the day after receipt.

If the firm is also still not in a position to issue a final response by the end of eight weeks, it should send a **holding response**, inform the Financial Ombudsman Service (FOS) and also inform the complainant of his right to complain directly to the Financial Ombudsman Service if he is not satisfied with the delay, and enclose a copy of the **FOS explanatory leaflet**.

A final response issued at any point during this process must inform the customer of his right to complain directly to the FOS and enclose a copy of the FOS explanatory leaflet.

Some firms operate a two-stage complaints procedure that provides for a complainant who is still not satisfied with the firm's initial response, to refer the matter back to the firm or to its head office.

These firms are subject to the time limits set out above, but the rules recognise that some complainants may never respond to the initial reply or may take a long time to do so. Therefore, where the firm sends a response to the complainant offering redress or explaining why they do not propose to give redress and setting out how the complainant can pursue the claim further within the firm or apply to the FOS, it is permissible for the firm to regard the matter as closed if the firm does not get a reply within eight weeks. If the complainant does reply indicating that they remain dissatisfied, then the general time limits will resume. However, the firm can discount any time in excess of a week taken by the complainant to reply.

Where a firm decides that redress is appropriate, a firm must provide **fair compensation** to the complainant. In addition, the FSA requires a firm to record complaints and report to the FSA every **six months** the total number received, the number completed within time scales and the total number outstanding. If no complaints were received the firm must still send a **nil return**.

6.1.2 Dealing with breaches

Section 150 FSMA 2000 creates a right action, in damages, for a **'private person'** who suffers loss as a result of contravention of certain rules by an authorised firm. A 'private person' means individuals not doing a regulated activity, and businesses, in very limited circumstances (where the loss does not arise from their business activities, e.g. setting up an occupational pension scheme for their employees).

This right exists in addition to common law actions, such as negligence or misrepresentation. However, S150 provides a privileged right of action since there is no need to prove negligence. It is sufficient that there has been a **rule breach** leading to **loss**.

S59 FSMA 2000 and the **Supervision Manual (SUP)** states that a person cannot carry out a controlled function in a firm unless that individual has been **approved** by the FSA. This requirement is expanded upon in the Authorisation Manual. Note that we are now referring to the individual members of staff on an authorised firm. If a person is performing a controlled function and is not approved, this is known as a breach of statutory duty and a private person has the right to sue their firm for damages if they have suffered loss, using **S71** FSMA 2000 (just as they have for a breach of rules under S150).

6.2 Financial Ombudsman Service (FOS)

A **complainant** must first go to the authorised firm being complained against. If the authorised firm does not resolve the complaint to his satisfaction, the complainant may refer it to the Ombudsman. The **Financial Ombudsman Service (FOS)** offers a cheap and informal method of independent adjudication of disputes between a firm and its customer. It is a body set up by statute and, while its Board is appointed by the FSA, it is entirely **independent** from the FSA and authorised firms. The FOS is, however, accountable to the FSA and is required to make an annual report to the FSA on its activities.

The FOS can consider a complaint against an authorised firm for an act or omission in carrying out any of the firm's regulated activities together with any ancillary activities that firm does. This is known as the **Compulsory Jurisdiction** of the FOS. In addition to the Compulsory Jurisdiction, the FOS can consider a complaint under its **'Voluntary Jurisdiction'**. This is where firms or businesses have submitted to the voluntary jurisdiction of the FOS by entering into a contract with the FOS. This is available, for example, to unauthorised firms and can cover activities such as advising on general insurance, deposit taking, loans, credit and debit card transactions and ancillary activities carried on by that voluntary participant where they are not regulated activities.

Only **eligible complainants** who have been customers of authorised firms or firms who have voluntarily agreed to abide by the FOS rules may use the Ombudsman system.

The FOS has set the following time limits beyond which it will not normally consider complaints.

- When **six months** have passed since the firm sent the consumer a final response
- When more than **six years** have passed **since the event** complained about, **or**
- More than **three years** since the person became aware of or could reasonably be expected to have become **aware** of the problem

After these time limits have expired, the firm complained about can choose to object to the Ombudsman looking at the complaint on the grounds that it is 'time-barred'.

If a **firm** misses a time limit, the FOS may move to the next stage of the complaint and may make provision for inconvenience or distress caused, in its award. If a complainant misses a time limit, the FOS may move to the next stage, or dismiss the complaint.

The Ombudsman may investigate the merits of the case and may also convene a hearing if necessary. Where the Ombudsman finds in favour of the complainant, it can force the firm to take appropriate steps to remedy the position including the payment of up to **£100,000 plus reasonable costs** (although awards of costs are not common). This figure will normally represent the financial loss the eligible complainant has suffered but can also cover any pain and suffering, damage to their reputation and any distress or inconvenience caused. If the Ombudsman considers that a sum greater than £100,000 would be fair, he can recommend that the firm pays the balance (although he cannot force the firm to pay this excess).

Once the Ombudsman has given a decision, the complainant may decide whether to accept or reject that decision. If the complainant accepts the decision, the authorised firm is bound by the decision. If the complainant rejects the Ombudsman's decision, they can pursue the matter further through the **courts**.

6.3 Financial Services Compensation Scheme (FSCS)

The **Financial Services Compensation Scheme** is designed to compensate **eligible claimants** where a relevant firm is unable or likely to be unable to meet claims against it. Generally speaking, therefore, the scheme will only apply where the firm is declared **insolvent or bankrupt**. The compensation scheme is independent, but accountable to the FSA and HM Treasury for its operations and works in partnership with the FSA in delivering the FSA's objectives, particularly that of consumer protection. The FSCS is funded by **levies** on authorised firms.

To seek compensation from the scheme, you must:

- Be an **eligible claimant**. This would generally cover most individuals (including, following August 2009 rule changes, directors of the failed entity and their close relatives, in respect of deposits) and small businesses. Broadly, an eligible claimant is defined as a claimant who is **not**:

  - A director or manager of the company in default, including their close relatives and individuals (except in the case of deposits – as outlined above)

  - A large company or large partnership/mutual association, as defined by UK Companies Acts limits, as amended from time to time

  - An authorised firm, unless they are a sole trader/small business and the claim arises out of a regulated activity of which they have no experience, i.e. do not have permission to carry out

  - An overseas financial services institution, supranational body, government and local authority

- Have a **'protected claim'**. This means certain types of claims in respect of deposits, insurance and investment business. Protected investment business means **designated investment business**, the activities of the manager/trustee of an authorised unit trust and the activities of the authorised corporate director/depository of an OEIC or ICVC. These activities must be carried on either from an establishment in the UK or in an EEA state by a UK firm who is passporting their services there.

- Be claiming against a **'relevant person'** who is in default. A relevant person means:

  - An authorised firm, except an EEA firm passporting into the UK (customers who lose money as a result of default by an EEA firm must seek compensation from the firm's home state system)

  - An appointed representative of the above

- Make the claim within the relevant **time limits** (normally six years from when the claim arose).

The FSA has extended, until 30 December 2010, its interim rules which allow separate compensation cover for customers with deposits in two **merging building societies**. The same extension has been made for customers who deposits are transferred from a failed firm to another deposit taker where they already have an account.

From **1 January 2010**, the maximum compensation levels were simplified, and are as follows. (Be sure to know the limit for protected investments, for your exam.)

	Limits (from 1 January 2010)
Protected investments and home finance	£50,000 (i.e. 100% of the first £50,000)
Protected deposits	£50,000 (i.e. 100% of the first £50,000)
Long-term insurance policies (for both UK and EEA risks)	90% of the claim
General insurance	100% for compulsory insurance; in other cases, 90% of the claim

The limits are per person and per claim, and not per account or contract held.

From 31 December 2010, the **Deposit Guarantee Schemes Directive (DGSD)**, will require payout of compensation within twenty days. The FSA is aligning its rules with that requirement but expects that payout will be faster, with a target of seven days.

The DGSD proposes a fully harmonised compensation limit set at €100,000 per authorised entity from 31 December 2010.

Consumer awareness of the FSCS will be promoted by a new rule which came into force on 1 January 2010, requiring firms to **provide information** on the existence of the **FSCS** and level of **protection** it offers to depositors, as well as proactively informing customers of any **additional trading names** under which the firm operates.

CHAPTER ROUNDUP

■ The Financial Services Authority is the single statutory regulator for the UK financial services industry. Unless exempt, firms undertaking regulated activities must be authorised (s19).

■ Firms and individuals must be careful about the possibility of laundering of the proceeds of crime. Failure to report laundering, and tipping off a money launderer, are offences.

■ Insider dealing is a criminal offence, and refers to acting with information that is not freely available to the market.

■ Insider dealing is one of various activities which may amount to market abuse – a civil offence.

■ The Data Protection Act imposes requirements on those holding personal data.

■ A firm must have appropriate procedures for dealing with complaints, and specified timescales for complaint handling must be followed. Complainants who are not satisfied with the firm's response may go to the Financial Ombudsman Service.

■ The Financial Services Compensation Scheme provides (limited) compensation in the event of a firm becoming insolvent.

Test Your Knowledge

Check your knowledge of the Chapter here, without referring back to the text.

1. Outline the four statutory objectives of the Financial Services Authority.

2. The general prohibition provides that no person may carry out regulated activities in the UK unless they are …………… to do so or are ……………….. *[Fill in the blanks]*

3. The general prohibition applies to 'persons'. 'Persons' here means:

   A   Individuals only
   B   Firms only
   C   Investment advice firms and their employees only
   D   Both individuals and firms

4. What are the five types of controlled function for which someone must be approved in order to perform?

5. Which one of the following is *not* one of the three typical stages of money laundering?

   A   Placement
   B   Layering
   C   Insider dealing
   D   Integration

6. If a firm's Money Laundering Reporting Officer suspects that money laundering has taken place, to which external agency should he normally report this?

7. It is an offence to disclose to any third party information which might prejudice an investigation into the laundering of the proceeds of drug trafficking, criminal conduct or of terrorist funds. What is this offence called?

8. What is the monetary limit for individual awards made by the Financial Ombudsman?

9. Hilary had investments of £39,000 at a financial institution when the institution became bankrupt. What is the maximum that she will normally recover through the Financial Services Compensation Scheme?

TEST YOUR KNOWLEDGE: ANSWERS

1. Market confidence: to ensure that the public can trust the soundness of the banking and financial system.

    Public awareness: to try to raise levels of financial literacy among the general public.

    Protection of consumers: the system recognises that there are several different types of consumers and seeks to deliver the appropriate levels of protection.

    Reduction of financial crime – from money laundering to insider dealing.

    See Section 2.2

2. The general prohibition provides that no person may carry out regulated activities in the UK unless they are authorised to do so or are exempt from authorisation.

    See Section 2.3

3. The general prohibition encompasses both individuals and firms.

    See Section 2.4

4. Governing functions; required functions; systems and control functions; significant management functions; customer functions.

    See Section 2.3

5. Placement, layering and integration are the three typical stages of money laundering, and so the option to choose is C.

    See Section 3.2

6. The Serious Organised Crime Agency.

    See Section 3.5.1

7. Tipping off.

    See Section 3.6

8. £100,000 plus reasonable costs.

    See Section 6.2

9. £39,000 × 100% = **£39,000** compensation is due.

    See Section 6.3

8

Taxation and Trusts

You are expected to understand the impact of income tax, capital gains tax and inheritance tax as they affect investments. This is potentially a topic with a great volume of detail, but you are only required to have a broad knowledge.

You should be aware of the rules on stamp duty, which is technically different from stamp duty reserve tax and stamp duty land tax.

You are also required to have an appreciation of trusts. In particular, their features and their uses.

CHAPTER CONTENTS

		Page
1	Income Tax	143
2	Capital Gains Tax	145
3	Inheritance Tax	145
4	Stamp Duty and Stamp Duty Reserve Tax	147
5	Personal Tax Rates and Allowance Summary	147
6	Value Added Tax (VAT)	148
7	Trusts	149
	Chapter Roundup	151
	Test Your Knowledge	153

CHAPTER LEARNING OBJECTIVES

Tax

- **Understand** the direct and indirect taxes as they apply to individuals:
  - Income Tax
  - Capital Gains Tax
  - Inheritance Tax
  - Stamp Duty and Stamp Duty Reserve Tax
  - VAT

- **Know** the main exemptions in respect of the main personal taxes

Trusts

- **Know** the features of the main trusts:
  - Discretionary
  - Interest in possession
  - Bare

- **Know** the definition of the following terms:
  - Trustee
  - Settlor
  - Beneficiary

- **Know** the main reasons for creating trusts

1 INCOME TAX

Understand the direct and indirect taxes as they apply to individuals: income tax
Know the main exemptions in respect of the main personal taxes

1.1 Who pays income tax?

Income tax is payable by all individuals and trusts **resident in the UK on their worldwide income**. Non-residents are only liable to income tax if they have a source of income derived in the UK.

1.2 Fiscal years

Income tax is calculated by reference to the **fiscal year**. This is also referred to as the income tax year or the year of assessment. The fiscal year runs from 6 April one year to 5 April the next year. The **fiscal year 2010/11** is the **year ending 5 April 2011**. The fiscal year 2011/12 starts on 6 April 2011.

Exam tip

> You do not need to know specific tax rates and allowances for the purpose of this exam. Where they are needed you will be given the relevant figures in the questions. The illustrations in this section use the **rates for 2010/11 as proposed in the March 2010 Budget**. Further changes may be made following the 2010 General Election.

1.3 Rates of income tax and the personal allowance

There are a number of allowable deductions an individual can make from gross income before tax is payable. The most important is the **personal allowance**. The personal allowance is deducted from the individual's total income, prior to arriving at his taxable income.

The full personal allowance is **£6,475** for the fiscal year 2010/11. However, this allowance is reduced by £1 for each £2 that an individual's adjusted net income exceeds £100,000. **Adjusted net income** is income less certain deductions such as pension contributions paid and gift aid charitable donations. Thus, someone with an adjusted net income of **£112,950 or more** gets no personal allowance.

Once any personal allowance has been deducted, the remainder of income (known as taxable income) is subject to income tax.

When determining the tax due, it is necessary to establish the gross taxable income however much of the income received is paid to us net i.e. after tax. Salaries are taxed when we receive them, as our employer is required to deduct Pay As You Earn (PAYE). Savings income is also usually taxed at source, but a company paying a dividend or coupon will not know the appropriate rate of tax each investor should pay. Therefore, we have a standard **withholding tax** of 20% on savings or interest income and 10% on dividends.

The rates of income tax applied to earned income, interest income and dividend income for 2010/11 are as follows.

Rate Band	Band Limits	Rate		
		Earnings	Interest	Dividends
Starting	£0 – £2,440	20%	10%	10%
Basic	£2,441 – £37,400	20%	20%	10%
Higher	£37,400 – £150,000	40%	40%	32.5%
Additional	Over £150,000	50%	50%	42.5%

Taxable income is taxed in a specific order: earnings first; interest second and dividends last. The starting rate is applied to the first £2,440 of taxable income, the basic rate is applied to the next £34,960 (£37,400 – £2,440), the higher rate is applied to the next £112,600 (£150,000 – £37,400), and the additional rate (new for 2010/11) on any taxable income above £150,000.

1.4 Savings and dividend income

Given that there is a standard withholding tax rate on savings income and dividends, tax may not have been deducted at the correct rate. The adjustment made in this situation is as follows.

	Savings income (20% withholding tax)	Dividend income (10% withholding tax)
Non-taxpayer	Reclaim 20% tax suffered	Cannot reclaim 10% tax suffered
Lower rate taxpayer	Can reclaim the additional 10% tax suffered	No more tax due
Basic rate taxpayer	No more tax due	No more tax due
Higher rate taxpayer	Extra 20% due, pay extra tax through year-end tax assessment	Extra 22½% due (making a total effective rate of 32½%) collected through year-end tax assessment
Additional rate taxpayer	Extra 30% due, pay extra tax through year-end tax assessment	Extra 32½% due (making a total effective rate of 42½%) collected through year-end tax assessment

Savings/interest income includes bank or building society account interest, as well as coupon payments received from both gilts and corporate bonds, but these are not usually subject to withholding tax. As such, the investor would be required to pay the full amount of tax that is appropriate.

Non-taxpayers can complete the **R85 form** which allows bank or building society interest to be paid gross, with no tax withheld at source.

Exam tip

You will not be asked to perform an income tax calculation in the exam.

BPP
LEARNING MEDIA

2 CAPITAL GAINS TAX

Understand the direct and indirect taxes as they apply to individuals: capital gains tax.
Know the main exemptions in respect of the main personal taxes.

2.1 Who pays capital gains tax?

Capital gains tax (CGT) is payable by **chargeable persons** on the **chargeable disposal** of a **chargeable asset**. A chargeable person is one who is **resident or ordinarily resident** in the UK

2.2 Assets chargeable to capital gains tax

An asset is a chargeable assets, unless it is covered by an exemption. Chargeable assets include items such as foreign currency, antiques, shares and other investments.

The **main exemptions** to be aware of are as follows.

- An individual's **principal private residence**, i.e. his or her main home

- **Gilts**

- **Qualifying corporate bonds**, i.e. non-convertible debt instruments issued by companies and denominated in sterling

- **Wasting assets**, i.e. ones that are always expected to fall in value as you use them, e.g. cars

- **Transfers** between husband and wife

2.3 Rates of capital gains tax and exemptions

Capital gains have the annual exemption deducted and are then subject to tax at a flat rate of 18%.

Entrepreneurs' relief allows the first £2 million of gains (a lifetime limit since 6 April 2008) from certain business asset disposals to be charged to CGT at a rate of 10%.

Capital losses from previous years can also be used to reduce the capital gain. Losses can be carried forward indefinitely until they have been used.

An **individual** is entitled to deduct an **annual exemption** of **£10,100** (2010/11).

Exam tip

> You will not be asked to perform a capital gains tax calculation in the exam.

3 INHERITANCE TAX

Understand the direct and indirect taxes as they apply to individuals: inheritance tax.
Know the main exemptions in respect of the main personal taxes.

3.1 Rates of inheritance tax

Inheritance tax (IHT) is charged, upon the death of an individual, at the rate of **40%** on the total value of the chargeable estate that exceeds £325,000 (2010/11). **The first £325,000 does not suffer any IHT**.

3.2 Potentially exempt transfers (PETs)

Any gifts made by an individual during their lifetime will be **exempt** from IHT, **unless they are made in the last seven years of the individual's life**, when they will be added to the chargeable estate. A lifetime gift is therefore potentially exempt from IHT until the seven-year period is over, when it becomes exempt. This rule prevents tax avoidance by disposing of one's property immediately prior to death.

Any IHT due, as a result of such a gift being added to the chargeable estate, will be payable by the **recipient of the gift**. The amount of tax due will vary depending on how long the donor survived after making the gift. If the donor died within three years of making the gift, IHT will be due at the full rate of 40%. If the donor died within three to seven years of the gift being made, the effective rate of IHT is reduced.

3.3 Exempt transfers whether made during life or on death

Regardless of the rules regarding PETs (discussed above) some transfers will be automatically exempt from inheritance tax, even if they are made within seven years of death. Some exemptions are available for lifetime transfers, whilst others are available whether the transfer was made during life or on death (i.e. in a will).

- **Gifts to spouses** – all gifts between husband and wife are always exempt from IHT, regardless of whether made during the donor's life or on death.

- **Gifts to charities** – all gifts to charities are exempt from IHT, regardless of whether made during the donor's life or on death. The charity must be a UK registered charity recognised by HMRC.

- **Gifts to political parties** – all gifts made to certain political parties are exempt from IHT, regardless of whether made during the donor's life or on death. A political party must satisfy certain requirements to enable the gift to be exempt. The party must have at least two MPs sitting in the House of Commons, or at least one MP and 150,000 votes at the last General Election.

- **Gifts to important national institutions** – all gifts made to important national institutions are exempt from IHT, regardless of whether made during the donor's life or on death. Important national institutions would include museums, such as the British Museum, and other well-known art galleries, libraries, etc.

- **Gifts for the public benefit** – this exemption, which applies to transfers during life or on death, applies to land and buildings which, in the opinion of the Treasury, are of outstanding scenic, historic or other interest. The transferee must be a non-profit making body and reasonable access for the public will usually be required.

- **Shares held in a qualifying trading company**, where the shares are traded on AIM or PLUS, are free from IHT and therefore not part of the chargeable estate, provided they have been held for two years or more at the time of death. This is because such shares qualify for Business Property Relief and so are not subject to IHT.

3.4 Exempt lifetime transfers

- **Small gifts exemption** – gifts made during the donor's lifetime (but not on death) not exceeding **£250 per recipient** per fiscal year are exempt from IHT. Any number of donees will qualify for this exemption in any one fiscal year. For example, ten gifts of £200 each in the fiscal year would all qualify for this exemption if made to different individuals.

- **Normal expenditure out of income** – where lifetime transfers can be shown to be habitual, made out of income and such that the donor's lifestyle will not be affected by the gift, they will be exempt from inheritance tax (e.g. a parent making regular premium payments into a life policy on behalf of his or her children, or just spending more than £250 on Christmas presents).

- **Gifts in consideration of marriage** – gifts made during an individual's lifetime (but not on death) in consideration of marriage are exempt from IHT. The amount of the exemption depends on who is making the gift. Gifts by a parent of the bride or groom are exempt up to £5,000. Gifts by a grandparent, great grandparent or even more remote ancestor are exempt up to £2,500. Gifts by anyone else are exempt up to £1,000.

3.5 Annual exemption

In addition to all other exemptions, any **gifts** made by an individual during their lifetime (but not on death) are **exempt** from IHT **up to £3,000 per fiscal year**. Should a particular gift be covered by another exemption, e.g. the small gifts exemption, then it does not use up the £3,000 annual exemption, which can be applied to other gifts.

The annual exemption is available for **carry forward for one year only**. For example, should an individual make no gifts over and above those covered by other exemptions in the fiscal year 2009/10, then that individual could make a total of £6,000 of gifts in the fiscal year 2010/11, all of which would be covered by the annual exemption.

4 STAMP DUTY AND STAMP DUTY RESERVE TAX

Understand the direct and indirect taxes as they apply to individuals: Stamp Duty and Stamp Duty Reserve Tax.

The purpose of **stamp duty** is to tax the **transfer of property** between individuals. The tax is payable by the **buyer** of, for example, **certificated shares** and is charged at a rate of **0.5%** of the consideration, **rounded up to the nearest £5**. Stamp duty is only paid by the purchaser and not the seller of shares. If the purchase involves **uncertificated** shares, the **Stamp Duty Reserve Tax (SDRT)** is payable by the buyer. SDRT is also charged at **0.5%** of the consideration, **rounded up to the nearest 1p**.

5 PERSONAL TAX RATES AND ALLOWANCE SUMMARY

	Income Tax	CGT	IHT
Annual exemption 2010/11	£6,475*	£10,100	£325,000
Starting rate (up to £2,440)	20% salary 10% dividends 10% other savings		
Basic rate (£2,440 – £37,400)	20% salary 10% dividends 20% other savings	Flat rate of 18%	Above £325,000, flat rate of 40%
Higher rate (£37,401 – £150,000)	40% salary 32½% dividends 40% other savings		
Additional rate (above £150,000)	50% salary 42½% dividends 50% other savings		

*reduced if adjusted net income exceeds £100,000

6 VALUE ADDED TAX (VAT)

Value Added Tax (VAT) is a tax businesses charge when they supply their goods and services in the United Kingdom (UK). If a business has paid VAT on goods in and then collected VAT on goods out, it pays the difference to HMRC. If the difference is negative then the business can reclaim this VAT from HMRC.

It is also charged on goods, and some services, that are imported from places outside the European Community (EC) and on goods and services coming into the UK from another EC Member State.

The following are examples of business supplies

- Selling new and used goods, including hire purchase
- Providing a service, for example, hairdressing and decorating
- Charging an admission price to go into buildings, or
- Self-employed people providing supplies, for example, some salesmen and subcontractors

There are three rates, as set out in the following Table.

Rate of VAT	Also known as	Applies to taxable supplies of
17.5%	Standard rate	Most goods and services
5%	Reduced rate	Certain fuel and power, energy saving materials, residential property works
0%	Zero rate	Certain goods and services on which you do not need to charge VAT

Taxable supplies on which the VAT rate is 0% include:

- Most food (but not meals in restaurants and cafes or hot take-away food and drink)
- Books
- Newspapers
- Children's clothing and shoes
- Exported goods
- Most prescriptions dispensed to a patient by a registered pharmacist
- Most public transport services

Individuals pay VAT when they make a purchase.

7   TRUSTS

7.1 What is a trust?

A trust arises when one person is the legal owner of property but owes a duty to exercise the rights of ownership for someone else's benefit. When an individual receives property 'on trust' for someone else, they are legally obliged to exercise their rights of ownership for the other person. In addition, the other person can enforce the obligation.

7.2 Participants in a trust

The **settlor** is the original owner of the property in question who creates a trust by transferring legal ownership of the property to the trustee. The settlor will have to say that the property is to be held in trust for one or more beneficiaries. The act of transferring property in this way is known as constituting the trust.

The **beneficiary** is the individual for whose benefit the property is being held. There may be one of more beneficiaries. The beneficiaries do not actually own the property but can ensure through the courts that the trust is administered correctly.

The **trustee** is the legal owner of the property and has control over the property settled in the trust. Of course, the trustee is obliged to manage the property for the beneficiaries in accordance with the terms of trust deed. The trust deed sets out the terms of the trust and the rights and duties of the participants in the trust.

7.3 Features of trusts

A trust may be a **bare** trust where there is a sole beneficiary. In such a trust, the trustee has no discretion over payment of income or capital to the beneficiary, who has an immediate and absolute right to both capital and income. The beneficiary can instruct the trustee how to manage the trust properly and has the right to take actual possession of the trust at any time.

An **interest in possession** trust arises where a beneficiary, known as a life interest or as an income beneficiary, has a legal right to the income or other benefit derived from the trust property as it arises. For example, the life interest may have the right to occupy a house during his or her lifetime. The income beneficiary might be entitled to receive income from trust property. Upon the death of the life interest or income beneficiary the assets will be held for the benefit of a second class of beneficiary known as the remainderman. The trustee therefore has a duty to safeguard the interests of both classes of beneficiary.

A **discretionary trust** exists where the trustee exercises their discretion as to which beneficiaries will be entitled to receive income or capital from the trust. This can be used to control the conduct of the beneficiaries by the trustee's use of discretionary powers. It also keeps the trust flexible. For example, the settlor may constitute a trust for the benefit of his/her grandchildren. If a new grandchild is born after the trust is set up, the grandchild will automatically rank as a beneficiary.

7.4 Why create a trust?

The purpose of many trusts is to enable the wealthy to retain their wealth. Trusts will tie up wealth within a family and will often be constructed to minimize tax liabilities.

Key benefits to families

- Controlling who owns and receives benefit from the property

- Potential reduction of tax liabilities

- Giving someone the benefit of property while preventing them from wasting it through careless actions

In such situations, the trustees may be members of the family or the family solicitor. Clearly there might be a conflict of interests so trust law defines the duties of the trustee very tightly.

CHAPTER ROUNDUP

- Income tax is payable by UK residents on their worldwide income.

- Capital Gains Tax (CGT) is now paid at a flat rate of 18%.

- Inheritance tax is charged on death. Lifetime gifts become exempt if they were made at least seven years before death. Various types of transfer are exempt.

- Stamp duly applies for share purchases.

- VAT is aimed at the end user/consumer of goods/services

- Trusts are created to protect family wealth and to prevent loss due to inappropriate actions.

TEST YOUR KNOWLEDGE

Check your knowledge of the Chapter here, without referring back to the text.

1. J is a non-taxpayer, K is a starting rate taxpayer, L is a basic rate taxpayer and M is a higher rate taxpayer. Each of them receives £10 in bank deposit interest. After all taxes are accounted for, which of the depositors, if any, receive the same post-tax amount from the interest?

    A   J and K only receive the same amounts
    B   K and L only receive the same amounts
    C   J, K and L only receive the same amounts
    D   J, K, L and M all receive different amounts

2. J, K, L and M (whose tax statuses are as in the previous question) each hold 100 shares in Green Bell plc, which pays a dividend of 10p. After all taxes are accounted for, which of the shareholders, if any, receive the same post-tax amount from the dividend?

    A   J and K only receive the same amounts
    B   K and L only receive the same amounts
    C   J, K and L only receive the same amounts
    D   J, K, L and M all receive different amounts

3. Give three examples of inheritance tax exemptions.

4. Sheila buys 200 shares in BZP plc at 555p. The trade settles through Euroclear UK & Ireland (CREST). What stamp duty reserve tax is payable by Sheila?

    A   £ Nil
    B   £5.55
    C   £10.00
    D   £11.10

5. The Beamingley Trust has a sole beneficiary. The trustee has no discretion over payment of income or capital to the beneficiary, who has an immediate and absolute right to both capital and income. The beneficiary can instruct the trustee how to manage the trust properly and has the right to take actual possession of the trust at any time. What kind of trust is this?

Test Your Knowledge: Answers

1.   The answer is D. All receive different amounts, as the tax rate on other savings is different for each.

     See Section 1.4

2.   The answer is C. The non-taxpayer J cannot reclaim the 10% tax credit.

     See Section 1.4

3.   You may have mentioned: gifts between spouses or civil partners, gifts to charities, gifts to certain political parties, gifts to certain national institutions or shares held in a qualifying trading company for more than two years.

     See Section 3.3

4.   SDRT is payable by the buyer, at 0.5% of the purchase consideration of £1,110, and so answer B is correct.

     See Section 4

5.   A bare trust.

     See Section 7.3

INDEX

Active fund management, 95
Additional rate tax, 144
Additional Voluntary Contribution (AVC)
    scheme, 79
Adjusted net income, 143
Alternative Investment Market (AIM), 36, 38
Annual Equivalent Rate (AER), 84
Annual exemption, 145, 147
Annual General Meeting (AGM), 29
Annual percentage rate (APR), 84
Approved persons, 123
Articles of Association, 28
Asset-backed securities (ABSs), 52
Assets Recovery Agency, 126
Assistance money laundering, 126
Association for Financial Markets in Europe, 13
Association of British Insurers (ABI), 12, 13
Association of Independent Financial Advisers
    (AIFA), 13
At best orders, 41
Authorisation (of firms), 121, 122
Authorised funds (types), 96

Balance of payments, 8
Bank loans, 83
Bank of England, 9, 119
Bank of England Act 1998, 119
Bare trust, 149
Basic rate tax, 144
Bears, 61
Beneficiary, 149
Bonds, 46
Bonus issues, 34
Box management, 95, 97
Breakeven point options, 66
British Bankers Association (BBA), 13
Building societies, 11
Bulls, 61
Buy-to-let investment, 78

Call option, 63
Cancellation price, 97
Capital gains tax, 145
Capital growth, 31
Capitalisation issues, 34
Capped rate mortgage, 86

Central counterparty, 40
Central counterparty service (CCS), 40
Central planning, 4
Certificates of Deposit (CDs), 54
CFA Institute, 13
Chargeable asset, 145
Chargeable disposal, 145
Chargeable persons, 145
Charges (unit trusts), 96
Chartered Institute for Securities & Investment
    (CISI), 13
Child Trust Fund (CTF), 112
Closed-ended schemes, 101
Collateralised bond obligation (CBO), 52
Collateralised debt obligation (CDO), 52
Collateralised loan obligation (CLO), 52
Commercial Paper, 54
Commercial property, 78
Committee of European Securities Regulators
    (CESR), 120
Commodities, 16
Companies Act 2006, 28
Compensation, 135
Complaints, 132
Consumer Prices Index (CPI), 7
Contracts For Difference (CfDs), 130
Convertibles, 51
Corporate actions, 33
Corporate bonds, 49
Coupon, 47
Covered options, 64
Credit card companies, 83
Credit creation, 6
Credit ratings (bonds), 50
Credit risk, 32
CREST, 43
Criminal Justice Act 1993 (CJA 1993), 125
Currency markets, 18
Current account (balance of payments), 8
Custodians, 12
Customer due diligence, 128

Dark liquidity pools, 20
Data Protection Act 1998, 131
Debt Management Office (DMO), 48
Deferred delivery, 61

Defined benefit pension schemes, 79
Defined contribution pension schemes, 79
Deflation, 7
Delivery versus payment (DVP), 32
Dematerialised settlement system, 43
Deposit Guarantee Schemes Directive, 136
Depositary, 100
Deposits, 76
Derivatives, 61
Deutsche Börse, 18
Dilution levy, 99
Discount – IT shares, 101
Discounted rate mortgage, 86
Discretionary trust, 149
Distribution channels, 20
Dividends, 31
Dual capacity, 42

Emerging market funds, 104
Enhanced due diligence (EDD), 128
Entrepreneurs' relief (CGT), 145
Equity shares, 29
Eurex, 16
Eurobonds, 50
Euroclear UK & Ireland (EUI), 32, 43
European Commission, 120
European Economic Area, 98
European Union, 5
Eurozone, 5
Event-driven funds, 104
Exchange rates, 5
Exchange-traded derivatives, 61
Exchange-traded funds (ETFs), 103
Execute and eliminate, 41
Execution only business, 21
Exempt lifetime transfers, 146
Exit charges, 96
ExtraMARK, 99
Extraordinary General Meeting (EGM), 29

Failure to report, 126
Fill or kill, 41
Final salary pension schemes, 79
Financial Ombudsman Service (FOS), 134
Financial Services Act 1986, 119
Financial Services and Markets Act 2000, 119
Financial Services and Markets Tribunal, 124
Financial Services Authority (FSA), 119
Financial Services Compensation Scheme
        (FSCS), 135
Fiscal year, 143

Fitch, 50
Fixed rate mortgage, 86
Fixed term account, 76
Flat yield, 52
Floating Rate Notes (FRN), 49
Foreign exchange, 18
Forward transactions, 19
FTSE indices, 38
Fund managers, 12
Fund supermarket, 100
Future, 62
Futures funds, 104

Gearing, 102
General prohibition, 122
Gilts, 46
Global macrofunds, 104
Government bonds, 46
Gross Domestic Product (GDP), 8

Hard commodities, 16
Hedge, 61
Hedge funds, 103
Higher rate tax, 144
Households, 4

ICE Futures Europe, 16
Income tax, 143
Income yield, 52
Independent Financial Advisers (IFAs), 20
Index tracker funds, 94
Indices, 38
Individual Savings Accounts (ISAs), 111
Industry trade bodies, 13
Inflation, 6
Inheritance tax, 145
Insider dealing, 129
Insurance companies, 12
Integration money laundering, 125
IntercontinentalExchange (ICE), 16
Inter-Dealer Brokers (IDBs), 11
Interest in possession trust, 149
Interest only mortgages, 86
Interest rate swap, 67
Interest yield, 52
International Capital Market Association, 13
Investment banks, 11
Investment bond, 82
Investment Companies with Variable Capital
        (ICVCs), 99, 100

Investment grade (bonds), 50
Investment Management Association (IMA), 13
Investment trusts (ITs), 94, 101
Invisible trade, 8
Issuer risk, 32

Layering, 125
LCH.Clearnet, 40
Lender of last resort, 10
LIBID, 53
LIBOR, 49, 53
Life assurance, 86
Liffe, 16
Limit orders, 41
Limited liability, 28
Liquidity risk, 32
Listing, 36
London Metal Exchange (LME), 16
London Stock Exchange (LSE), 14
Long call, 65
Long put, 66
Long/short funds, 103

Macroeconomics, 4
Mandatory quote period (MQP), 43
Market abuse, 130
Market economy, 5
Market makers, 42
Market orders, 41
Market risk, 32
Market-neutral funds, 103
Markets in Financial Instruments Directive
    (MiFID), 5, 120
Memorandum of Association, 28
Mergers, 36
MiFID, 42
Mixed economy, 5
Monetary Policy Committee, 9
Money laundering, 125
Money Laundering Directives, 125
Money Laundering Regulations 2007, 129
Money Laundering Reporting Officer, 126
Money market instruments, 53
Money purchase pension schemes, 79
Moody's, 50
Mortgages, 85
Multilateral Trading Facilities (MTFs), 20

NASDAQ, 18
National Association of Pension Funds (NAPF),
    12
Net asset value (NAV), 94
New York Stock Exchange (NYSE), 18
Nil paid values, 36
Nominee, 44
Non-investment grade (bonds), 50
Non-UCITS retail scheme (NURS), 96
Novate, 40
NYSE Euronext, 18
NYSE Liffe, 16

Occupational pension schemes, 79
Offer for sale, 15
Offshore bonds, 83
Offshore funds, 97
Open economy, 5
Open-Ended Investment Companies (OEICs), 94,
    99
Option, 63
Order book, 40
Ordinary shares, 29
OTC derivatives, 61
Overdrafts, 83

Passive fund management, 95
Pay As You Earn (PAYE), 143
Pension funds, 11
Pension mortgage, 86
Pension schemes, 79
Personal allowance, 143
Personal pension plans (PPs), 80
Placement, 125
Placing, 15
Platforms, 18, 20, 100
Politically exposed persons (PEPs), 128
Potentially exempt transfers (PETs), 146
Pre-emption rights, 34
Preference shares, 30
Premium – IT shares, 102
Premium (options), 63
Premium listing, 37
Price risk, 32
Primary market, 14
Principles-based regulation, 123
Private companies, 28
Proceeds of Crime Act 2002 (POCA 2002), 125
Professional (wholesale) market, 20
Professional bodies, 13

Property, 78
Protected claim, 135
Proxy, 29
Public companies, 28
Public Sector Net Cash Requirement (PSNCR), 9, 48
Put option, 63

Qualified investor scheme (QIS), 96

R 85, 76, 144
Real Estate Investment Trusts (REITs), 104
Recognised Clearing House (RCH), 43
Recognised investment exchange, 36
Registrar, 45
Registrar of companies, 28
Repayment mortgages, 85
Residential property, 78
Retail banks, 10
Retail clients, 20
Retail Prices Index (RPI), 6
Rights issue, 34
Risk-based approach (to regulation), 123
Risks (shares), 32
RPIX, 7
Running yield, 52

Scrip issues, 34
SEAQ, 42
Secondary market, 14
Secured borrowing, 85
Securities houses, 11
Securitisation, 52
Self Invested Personal Pension (SIPP), 80
Self-regulating organisations, 119
Self-regulation, 119
Serious Organised Crime Agency (SOCA), 126
SETS, 40
SETSqx, 42
Settlor, 149
Share benefits, 32
Share price indices, 38
Shareholders, 29
Short call, 66
Short put, 67
Simplified due diligence (SDD), 128
Single Life Assurance Premium Bonds, 82
Small Self Administered Schemes (SSAS), 80
Société d'investissement à capital variables (SICAVs), 100

Soft commodities, 16
Speculator, 61
Split capital investment trusts, 102
Sponsor (listings), 38
Sponsored members (of CREST), 45
Spot market (forex), 19
Stakeholder pension plans (SHPs), 80
Stamp duty, 147
Stamp duty reserve tax, 147
Standard & Poor's, 50
Standard listing, 37
Starting rate tax, 144
State controlled economy, 4
State pension (basic), 79
State Second Pension (S2P), 79
Statutory objectives (of FSA), 121
Statutory regulation, 119
Stock Transfer Form, 33
Stockbrokers, 11

Table A, 28
Takeover, 36
Tax Incentivised Savings Association, 13
Term assurance, 87
Theoretical ex-rights price, 35
Third party administrators, 12
Tied advisers, 20
Tokyo Stock Exchange, 18
Tracking error, 94
Treasury bill, 54
Treating customers fairly (TCF), 123, 124
Trustee, 95, 149
Trusts, 149

UCITS, 98
UCITS scheme, 96
UK listing authority, 36
Underwriting, 36
Unemployment, 9
Unit trusts, 94, 95
Unit-linked policies, 87
Unregulated funds, 96
Unsecured borrowing, 85
User members (of CREST), 45

Value Added Tax (VAT), 148
Variable rate mortgage, 86
Visible trade, 8
Voting rights, 31

Whole of life assurance, 87
Withholding tax, 143
With-profit policies, 87

Zero-coupon bonds, 51